The Relationship Cure & Couples Guide for Loving Relationships

Don't Settle for the Crumbs When You Can Have the Whole Cake

Dr. Randee Anderson

The Relationship Cure & Couples Guide for Loving Relationships
Don't Settle for the Crumbs When You Can Have the Whole Cake

Randee Anderson

Published by TrueLovePublications.net

ISBN 978-0692867778

Disclaimer: The information and ideas in this book are for educational purposes only. This book is not intended to be a substitute for consulting with an appropriate health care provider. The authors and publisher disclaim any liability arising directly or indirectly from this book.

Dedication

I would like to thank my husband Tim, man of grace and total support. You love completely and fill my being with comfort. Thank you to Corey, son of my soul. You are incredibly kind and a treasure since the day you were born. Thank you to Cassie, daughter of my heart. You are so sweet and possess great gifts and lovely energy.

I would like to thank all of my lovely clients who shared their stories, their lives and their souls with me. You all have been so brave. You have struggled so and changed behaviors beautifully. You were vulnerable, open and so caring. Thank you for trusting me and sharing your pain. You made my goal of helping people come to fruition. You never gave up when the going got rough.

Thank you, also, to my family of origin. To the souls of my parents who taught me through sadness as well as joy how to be in this world. Without their function and dysfunction, I would not have been able to grow. To my sister, Amy and my brother, Terry. I'm so glad to know you for who you are and like you not just because we're related.

Finally, I would like to thank Howard VanEs and his team at Let's Write Books, Inc. for their expert guidance and hand-holding during the publishing process for this book.

Table of Contents

Introduction

Jan has just finished telling Mark about her terrible boss: how he overworks her, talks about everyone behind their backs, and sets deadlines that are impossible to meet. Mark just nods his head and then turns back to the newspaper. Jan growls, "You never listen to me!" and storms out of the room.

***

Stan comes home from a long day at work, just longing to lie down on the couch and catch the last inning of the baseball game. But when he walks in the door, he's met with a glare from his fiancée, Leann. Stan knows this look well. What did I do this time? he wonders, waiting for the lecture. Usually, it's something he was "supposed" to know, do or remember. Stan feels confused, like he's caught in some twisted trivia game where he never knows the correct answer.

***

Steve and Linda love talking. In fact they never stop! They are both fond of sharing their stream-of-consciousness with each other at all times, including criticisms of what the other person "should" do in any given situation. Many times, they're so busy talking that they never hear what the other person is saying. This leads to frequent fights, lengthy talks afterward and a shaky sense of calm before the next storm erupts.

When they work, relationships can be wonderfully supportive, loving and life-affirming. In a healthy, positive relationship, both people are free to be themselves and they nurture the partnership in such a way that it brings out the best in the other person. Though most of us would love to be involved in this type of relationship, this is not the case for the majority of people. Unfortunately, too many relationships today are absolutely demanding, draining and frustrating.

If any of these scenarios resonated with you—and even if they did not— there are probably some or many aspects of your relationship that you would like to improve or change. "Difficult" relationships are very common and through my twenty-five years of experience as a licensed marriage, family and individual therapist specializing in couples therapy, I've seen it all. People have come to me because they are unhappy in their relationship, they're looking for a better relationship or they're wondering if they should end the one they are in currently.

No matter what your present situation may be, this book can help. Maybe you're depressed or anxious and your relationships are suffering. Maybe you're constantly second-guessing yourself and feel diminished like you're never good enough. Or perhaps you:

- Feel unhappy that you have no voice in your relationship
- Repeat the same patterns over and over with your significant other
- Feel frustrated in a relationship
- Are unsure of what your partner wants
- Are not getting your needs met
- Fight constantly with your partner, or
- Experience frequent dissatisfaction with your relationship.

This book is an experiential journey that will walk you through the "hows" of learning how to get your needs met from those you love. So often we were raised not to honor our feelings; instead, we were taught to intellectualize … or just "suck it up." Basically, we were told to do anything other than acknowledge (let alone feel) whatever emotions we were experiencing at the time.

"Children are to be seen and not heard" is the motto of many past generations. Although this ideal hasn't translated into emotionally healthy adults, our parents—and their parents—raised us as best they could. They bought into those ingrained ideas and therefore perpetuated dysfunctional behaviors.

All of us have received negative messaging from our parents at one time or another. None of us has been parented perfectly (nor the preceding generations) so we live under the strong influence of largely unspoken dysfunctional behaviors. These patterns, unless interrupted, can continue as we tend to practice the habits of our past parenting completely unconsciously. This is why some level of dysfunction is unavoidable. However, it is possible to normalize those messages and learn how to stop reacting in the same dysfunctional ways from the past. By differentiating and separating those messages you can open the door to becoming your authentic self: you decide which historical messages to keep and which messages you may let go. Instead of blindly following what was demonstrated by your family, you will learn how to listen to and follow your own path. Interestingly, the more you do this, the more easily you can cultivate authentic and loving relationships with *everyone* in your life—from your significant other to your family, friends and even your coworkers.

Consider this: if you come from a family that did not communicate much with each other—especially when it came to feelings—then you are not going to know how to express what you need. You'll find yourself saying, "I don't know how I feel and I don't know what I think." This doesn't make you a difficult client or horrible person. Your family's style of interaction has simply shaped your interpersonal style in such a way that potentially blocks communication in your important relationships. If this describes you then you may have heard "Because I said so!" or

"Because I'm the parent!" frequently during your childhood. That's because this parental response is typical when a child asks a question that relates to feelings and the family is uncomfortable addressing, discussing and dealing with their feelings.

No matter what your family dynamics were, it is vital to identify them and work from there in order to elicit true change. Otherwise you are likely to continue to carry those dysfunctional patterns with you into every relationship. You will wonder why you run into difficulties with each new person you meet—no matter how hard you try to make the relationships work.

Self-help books are wonderful tools and we often relate beautifully to the concepts they present. We can recognize our patterns and truly believe the book was written just for us. Unfortunately, many of these books don't show us *how* to implement these new concepts being discussed or *how* to actually do things differently. This book is different: I want to give you the hands-on methods and practices that will allow you to change your thoughts and behaviors, and which will subsequently improve your relationships.

It's important to note that feelings don't have time clocks and they don't have intellect, so you could be feeling something from ten years ago—or two days ago. With this book, I will help you work with those feelings to *stop the dysfunction*. I want to put an end to the negative messaging and resulting behaviors that have been passed down through the generations. Let's stop it here and prevent it from surfacing in the future!

If you are currently in a relationship, you may be thinking: *Yes, but if I change and my partner doesn't want to, how will that help? Doesn't it take two to tango?* While it is ideal for both partners to work through this book and individually make changes, this may not be the reality for you. You might have a partner who is not exactly in sync with you and motivated at this time to find new or better ways of relating. The good news is that an interesting phenomenon takes place even when only one person makes changes to his or her life: as that person changes, the entire relationship takes on a new dynamic. Sometimes this results in the other person changing—and many times, that person isn't even aware of those changes taking place because it happens very organically. Other times, the person who is evolving into a better version of him- or herself isn't bothered by some of the same pet peeves from the past. What he or she once perceived as an issue is no longer quite so important.

As you read this book and move through the exercises I will work with you at three different levels:

1. Intra-psychically (how you individually think, feel and behave)
2. Inter-personally (how you are in relationships) and
3. Multi-generationally (what you learned and still *do* from your family of origin that does or does not serve you well).

Imagine being in a relationship where you enjoy the other person's company and look forward to spending time together ... where you feel good about yourself ... where you feel validated and listened to ... and where you are able to love deeply and passionately. Though you might think this is the Hollywood version of the "perfect relationship," I'm here to tell you that it really is very possible to use the approaches in this book to:

- Feel more content
- Learn how to communicate your needs effectively
- Improve your current (and future) relationships
- Get more of the love you need and want
- Experience less conflict in relationships
- Let go of old emotional wounds and
- Have more confidence in yourself and the way you interact with others.

Were you taught to believe it was selfish to ask for what you need? If so, I will show you how unselfish meeting your needs truly is. I want to show you how to not merely settle for 10, 20 or even 30 percent of happiness, just because you think it is better than nothing—or better than being alone. I will give you the tools so you know how to get your needs met and still be in loving relationships. I want to show you how much more effective your life will become if you are living in contentment. You deserve to be loved the way you need; don't settle for crumbs when you can have the whole cake!

So, if you're looking forward to a life that is happier, healthier, more fulfilling and more loving, then get ready, because it's time to learn *how* to do just that! We will begin with *The Bucket Theory* so you can learn how to jump-start the process of getting your emotional needs met in a healthy, positive way.

HOW TO GET THE MOST FROM THIS BOOK

This book is filled with practical exercises that will enhance your learning and cement new relationship behaviors to make the changes you are looking for. To make a change in your behavior you have to DO the exercises. They are designed to give you an experience of doing things differently. In order to get the most benefit, make sure you follow my three simple "rules."

1. There is no good or bad or wrong or right. There are just different ways of doing things.
2. Avoid the word "should." It is always used as a value judgment that one person has for another.
3. When it comes to answering a question there is no "I don't know" because that usually means "I'm not going to take the time to think about it."
4. When you stick to the rules your journey of personal discovery will be enlightening, exciting and enriching and will put you on the road to healthier, happier relationships.

Chapter 1
The Bucket Theory

"Knowing yourself is the beginning of all wisdom."

- Aristotle

I believe everyone is born with an invisible bucket inside of them. Your mom hurts your feelings and you put that feeling in the bucket. You feel hurt by your friend or your spouse and you put that feeling in the bucket. At a certain point in time the bucket becomes full. You take one more feeling, it goes in the bucket and the bucket overflows. That is usually the moment when people seek therapy.

The bucket is a great metaphor for the way feelings are stored as a result of certain experiences. Feelings don't have time clocks or intellect, so you may be experiencing a feeling from ten years or two days ago. The most challenging of life's experiences is to feel difficult feelings. It is very common to believe that to cry is a sign of weakness. However, what many people don't realize—and contrary to popular opinion—is that when you allow yourself to feel you are at your strongest.

So in your bucket you are very likely to find hurt, sadness, disappointment, anxiety, etc., and you don't know what to do with those feelings. And because what was put into the bucket was never really addressed, you finally must face those feelings and deal with them in order to begin to feel better. In the meantime it's quite probable that those unwieldy emotions are affecting your relationships as well. All of the hurt, sadness, disappointment and anger that is overflowing needs to go somewhere, and it usually becomes directed at others.

Your bucket can be filled with feelings from years and years ago. If you didn't take the time to experience and process your feelings at the time, they have simply accumulated in the bucket.

Maybe your bucket hasn't overflowed—yet. On the other hand, perhaps your bucket has been overflowing and flooding your life with difficult emotions and feelings for a long time. No matter where you are in your journey, understand that it is imperative to acknowledge the feelings in your bucket. The sooner you handle and heal these feelings, the sooner you will position yourself to operate positively both inside yourself as well as with others in your life. Unfortunately, most people are not taught how to deal with difficult feelings. However, with a little patience, practice and tools from this chapter and book, you will be well on your way to emptying your bucket.

As you begin to recognize the feelings that you've poured into your invisible bucket, please do not judge yourself for not taking care of it earlier in life. Richard Stine, the famous artist and writer once said, "It is simple … We are where we are, doing what we should be doing, otherwise we would be somewhere else doing something else." If you had known at the time what you do now, you would have made a different decision. Next, remind yourself—because this bears repeating frequently—that feelings don't have time clocks. Feelings don't have intellect either, otherwise they would be thoughts and not feelings.

PAIN FROM THE PAST: IT FEELS SO REAL

Feelings have a particular type of magic. If you call to mind an extremely painful or pleasurable experience from your past, you can probably still feel the same way you felt during the actual experience—even if the experience occurred years ago.

Think back to a joyful event in your life: maybe it was the birth of a child, achieving an important accomplishment, getting married, or getting some kind of award. Can you feel the excitement? The anticipation? The happiness?

The same goes for negative experiences. Think back to a time that you found out someone died, you lost a job or a relationship came to an end. How did you feel? Did you process these feelings initially? Or were they acknowledged or ignored?

I can still feel today the horror of my mother's struggle with cancer. I can still feel the pain, despair and fear—even though this happened decades ago. Although time constantly moves forward, our feelings don't necessarily keep pace. No matter how long ago you felt them it is crucial to your personal growth and emotional well-being to experience, feel and honor your feelings. Through this process you will nurture yourself and ultimately improve all of your relationships. Without all of those negative "overflow" emotions that once overwhelmed you, you will begin to experience a lightness, calmness and clarity that not only makes you feel better and empowered, but also translates into more positive interactions with the people in your life. Once the bucket begins to empty, we learn how to replace the negative messages with messages that are life-affirming, nurturing and positive.

There is a common belief that if you don't access, accept and honor your feelings, your body is going to do everything it can to *force* you to feel. Ulcers, anxiety, panic attacks, obsessions and depression are just a few of the manifestations of unfelt emotions. When you were an infant you experienced discomfort through fear, tactile needs, hunger, cold, and so on. And, if your parents didn't know what you needed every time you cried—which is common, since parents don't know what to do *every single time*—they might not have given you the nurturing you craved to feel better. Even if they picked you up, fed you, caressed you and soothed you, that might not have been exactly what you needed in the moment. Most parents would think they were doing the right thing, and they probably had your best interests at heart. But all of us are fallible and whenever your parents failed to *honor* your feelings—or couldn't teach you how to handle them—you probably figured out how to deal with your emotions on your own. You might have even interpreted your parents' actions and arrived at your own conclusions about their intentions and what "should" be done.

For instance, in my life, I learned early on how to intellectualize my feelings because that's how my mother handled her own uncomfortable feelings. I vividly recall approaching her as a teenager; I was extremely upset because the boys in school had been making fun of my height. Feeling quite raw, I told my mother how I felt. Rather than honor my feelings of isolation and embarrassment, she lovingly said, "Don't worry, they're just jealous. When you're older, you can join the tall club." Later, when I approached her because I felt my nose was too big, she again said lovingly, "Don't worry, you can get a nose job when you're older."

I use the word "lovingly" because I do believe that her intention came from a loving place, albeit an ineffective one. Obviously, my mother's response did nothing to care for the way I felt. I not only learned to *not* honor my feelings, I learned to intellectualize them. Her approach was to "fix it" and come up with a solution that would "solve" the problem.

Mary was another person who was raised by loving parents, but their value system demanded that she always be the "good girl." That meant being a constant people-pleaser, even if it meant stuffing negative emotions down deep inside where no one could see or know how she really felt. Through the years, filling her bucket with painful emotions became second nature to her, so the bucket eventually overflowed.

Right after college graduation, Mary married her college sweetheart. Most of the time Mary and Ron got along well, but Ron had a habit of being chronically late that drove Mary nuts! Her people-pleasing nature wouldn't allow Mary to address her anger and disappointment every time Ron failed to pick her up at an appointed time or miss family get-togethers and date nights because he was running behind on a project at work or around the house. So, Mary would silently fret and fume until she reached breaking point. One day when Ron was running late again for dinner and a movie, Mary exploded. She ranted and raved and stormed out of the house, but not before telling Ron she wanted a divorce.

Ron couldn't believe his ears. In his mind, Mary was making a mountain out of a molehill. Couldn't she see that he was just an hour behind? Plus, he was fixing the leaky faucet, so wasn't she grateful that he was making improvements around the house? Most guys Ron knew spent their Sunday afternoons on the couch, watching ball games. How could she be angry with him for this?

Many of us were raised like Mary—with this "no feeling" rule. It is time to stop this vicious cycle of not feeling by honoring ourselves, stating our feelings and sharing them so that our children—and generations to come—can do the same.

The big question is *how?* How do you access your feelings and honor them? Throughout this book, you will identify the feelings that are in your own personal bucket (and at what age you put them there). The corresponding exercises for each chapter will help you learn to honor those feelings.

Part of the process will be to identify if these feelings are in fact your own. Often children, especially young ones, "sponge" feelings from family and friends and make those emotions their own, even when the situation and resultant feelings have nothing whatsoever to do with them. This can happen if you witnessed any form of injustice, watched someone get shamed, were abused, were treated unfairly and the list goes on. Maybe you are super sensitive, and if you saw your mother crying, you also felt sad. Or in friendships, you didn't want to watch your friend get hurt, so you took on the suffering. All of these situations can lead to you sponging feelings off of others and internalizing them because you aren't sure how to separate yourself from that person. These are what I call "triggered feelings" because they belong to other people but you still feel them. Over time, you risk losing the ability to tell which feelings are your own.

Fortunately, when Mary had a chance to sit with her feelings and admit how angry and disappointed she felt every time Ron was late, things began to change. By honoring her own feelings, Mary exposed those negative emotions to the light of day. Interestingly, the feelings weren't as scary as she had originally thought. She realized that the more she tried to please everyone and ignore the way she felt, the worse she ended up treating Ron. At that moment, she knew in her heart that her threat to divorce him was simply a reaction to years of refusing to acknowledge the way she felt. Though she didn't change overnight, Mary knew she was finally on the path to admitting how she really felt—and that it was OK to feel her feelings, too!

EXERCISE: THE FEELINGS BUCKET

Today, you will begin to gently identify feelings that have been hidden so that as you move forward you can re-feel and heal the feelings from your bucket. Later, you will also learn how to identify the triggers that activate some of your bucket feelings.

Please be kind and patient with yourself as you identify these feelings. Realize that for now all I want you to do is write them down. Further on in the process there will be a time for you to re-feel the emotions. To be clear, the goal in this exercise is to begin identifying what's *in* the bucket. As you get stronger, you will be able to confront and embrace your feelings without fear.

STEPS:

1. Gather the following supplies: a pen or pencil, bucket (or other container) and slips of paper or index cards.
2. Sit quietly and think of a situation you experienced recently that brought up negative feelings. For example, if your best friend called at the last minute and canceled the plans the two of you had, write the situation down on a slip of paper.
3. Next, name the feeling you felt as a result of the situation. In this case, you might have felt disappointed. Write "disappointed" on the paper underneath your description of the experience.
4. Drop the paper into the bucket.
5. Continue to think about the *same* emotion—in this case it would be disappointment—and describe another time that you felt disappointed. Maybe your partner

was supposed to take the kids somewhere special, was called into work and was unable to follow through on the agreed commitment. After you write that situation down, drop that paper into the bucket too.

6. Repeat step 5, recording the similar feeling and associated event until you can't think of any more. Many times, you will remember circumstances and experiences from childhood. Write them down, too!

7. You may notice that even while you are reading this book that feelings in your bucket may be triggered or you have experiences that you want to apply this process to. You can process those feelings so that your relationships are, and continue to be healthy.

We are in the "identification" stage, so simply acknowledging all of the times you felt this particular emotion is sufficient. If you are up to it, however, you may wish to continue to repeat this exercise with a new emotion and other relevant situations. For example, maybe you are thinking of times you were afraid or sad or anxious.

If you experience a visceral response or start to cry while completing this exercise, most likely you have been carrying that feeling around in the bucket for a while. You may even find that you don't even want to write the feeling down. This is a sign you are probably blocking that feeling and it might be too painful to re-feel today. In that instance, please, immediately write the feeling on the page, but do not go any further with examples that relate to it. This list is your first step in preparing to empty the bucket. The healing will come later, so don't worry if you can't go deeper at this time.

As you write, you will probably begin to notice some feelings of lightness and clarity that arise with releasing these burdens onto paper. This is the important first step. Of course, we haven't completely dealt with the feelings yet—that's why the bucket is still "full"!—but just the act of recording your experiences and feelings should spark a feeling of release (and maybe catharsis) which plays an important role.

Chapter 2
Death by Triangulation

"The roles we play in each other's lives are only as powerful as the trust and connection between us—the protection, safety, and caring we are willing to share."

- Oprah Winfrey

Marianne storms into her son's bedroom, carrying a huge duffel bag. "Ben, I told you that this soccer bag was supposed to be emptied yesterday! How am I going to have your uniform clean for the tournament if it's rotting in this dirty, smelly bag?"

Ben looks up at his mother from his cell phone. Instantly, his eyes well up with tears. "Mom, I forgot! And I was so busy studying for my Bio test that it just slipped my mind."

Meanwhile, Marianne's husband overhears the argument as he passes by the bedroom door. He pops into the room and says: "Marianne, it's not such a big deal. Look, I can wash those clothes, and they'll be dry in plenty of time for tomorrow's game." While Marianne's back is turned, Joe smiles at his son and winks.

Marianne turns to Joe and snaps: "Just stay out of this, Joe! How is Ben ever going to learn how to be responsible if you keep stepping in to save the day?"

For most of us, the very same people we needed to serve as role models for appropriate, healthy communication skills were the same people who could not provide the necessary guidance. Why? Because we were all in the same boat together—floundering around without knowing what was wrong with our own communication skills. Negative patterns have taken root and many of them have been passed on generationally. In response, we rely on dysfunctional methods of coping. Psychologist Dr. Stephen Karpman has terms this "The Karpman Triangle."[1]

In the Karpman Triangle, people tend to fall into one of three roles—victim, rescuer and/or perpetrator (originally termed "persecutor"). Many of these roles are established early on in the family of origin. Over time, everyone learns his or her "assigned" role—and becomes accustomed to acting and reacting within those roles. Not only that, people learn to play their assigned roles well! In the example above, Ben learned how to play the role of *victim* whenever his mother became the *perpetrator*, causing Ben's father to serve as the *rescuer* and save Ben from those uncomfortable conflicts. Eventually, Ben is going to generalize his role to all situations, both within and outside of his family. That means he might perceive any conflict as an attack and he could automatically regress into that practiced innocent, persecuted victim who can't help himself.

Now, let's fast-forward to when it comes time for Ben to leave home as an adult. He might be thinking, "Finally, I'm going to be loved the way I need to be." Unfortunately, the chances of this happening are slim, because Ben is most likely going to recreate the role he became accustomed to in childhood—except with different people. In this case, Ben (as the victim) will continue to search for a rescuer who will help

---

1   Karpman, S. (n.d.). The Official Site of the Karpman Drama Triangle. Retrieved October 3, 2015, from http://www.karpmandramatriangle.com

ease his pain and discomfort. In fact, there's an exceptional chance that he will gravitate toward romantic partners who demonstrate an excessive concern for Ben's well-being—to the point that Ben won't need to be responsible for his own feelings and circumstances. Or, he may partner with people who are more aggressive, since the perpetrator-victim dynamic feels so comfortable to him.

The emotionality of a triangle causes guilt or shame in the family system. Guilt is based on the notion that "I *did* or *said* something bad," while shame is based on the perception that "I *am* bad." Clearly, these emotions are powerful and only lead to more dysfunction.

ROLE CALL

What role are you playing? Are you, like Ben, accustomed to being a victim? Or are you more like Marianne the perpetrator or Joe the rescuer? Read the descriptions and examples below of each role in the Karpman Triangle and see if you can relate to any of them. Please note that these roles occur in all aspects of our lives—marriage, friendship and even in the workplace.

Role playing is contextual and depends on the situation and person. We tend to move from role to role. So while you may sometimes act like a perpetrator, you may also play the victim and rescuer at other times. In Ben's situation, he may seek dominance over his mom by criticizing her. This puts him in the power position of the perpetrator. At other times he might play the part of rescuer if he were to stand up for a friend who is being bullied at school. Regardless of the dynamic nature of these roles, there is one primary role that you are most closely aligned with, and this predominant role is the one with which you are most comfortable and operate within most frequently.

Identifying your primary role is the key and the first step to "de-triangulate" yourself from dysfunction.

Here are the roles:

ROLE #1: THE PERPETRATOR

This role is difficult to identify in yourself because if you are a perpetrator, you are usually so intent on getting other people to agree with you, listen to you and do what you want that you're not even aware that you're being the perpetrator. However, here are some key attributes and traits that may hint that you are behaving in this way. Perpetrators are typically:

- Rude
- Judgmental
- Critical
- Angry
- Impulsive (acting and speaking before thinking)
- Unfiltered
- Mean
- Accusatory.

For example, Susan (the perpetrator) lived in an apartment building that had a centrally controlled thermostat. She would often turn up the temperature—even though the other tenants didn't necessarily want it or like it. Another tenant, Amy (the victim), would become angry because Susan wasn't considering how the other people felt about changing the thermostat. Jacquelin, Amy's friend (the rescuer), who also lived in the building decided to approach Susan. She said, "Susan, could you please let the building owner control the temp? I'm sorry, I'm just not OK with how warm it is in the building all the time."

At this, Susan responded with, "Well, I pay rent, too! I'm entitled to living comfortably, so I really don't care if you're OK with it or not. In fact, you keep yourself so bundled up in jackets and sweaters that it's no wonder you're hot! You know, maybe you're going through menopause early and you're having hot flashes." And on it went.

Note that most perpetrators use a lot of "you" language: "You should do this." "You should think that." "Why do you always …?" "You never …" and so on. Essentially, they spend most of their time blaming others.

In romantic relationships this can translate to constant nagging, criticizing and belittling. The partner, in turn, will become a very defensive victim. With time, the victim may get tired of all the attacks and attempt to get back at the perpetrator by rebelling in some form (purposely not doing what the perpetrator wants, arguing back, leaving the relationship, cheating, etc.).

ROLE #2: THE VICTIM

To be the victim there needs to be a perpetrator, so people who were victims as a child tend to gravitate toward people who will play this dominant role, along with people who will rescue them. Of course, they aren't consciously trying to put themselves into situation in which they feel diminished or criticized. However, their repeated experiences as a victim create a dysfunctional comfort level with these negative circumstances.

Victims usually:

- Feel they lack control over their circumstances
- Have low self-esteem
- View others as stronger and more confident
- Believe that people are out to get them
- Feel paranoid, worried and anxious
- View life as a series of events based on good or bad luck
- Find security in other people who protect them

Kaitlyn was constantly criticized and judged by her parents. As an only child, she was the first and last for everything, and this put tremendous pressure on her to excel at all times. So, if she were a few minutes late after curfew, she was belittled for being irresponsible—and then grounded for months. However, when she tried to behave more maturely by reprimanding her younger cousins for not following the rules, her parents would berate her for trying to "be the parent." They would accuse Kaitlyn of erroneously taking things into her own hands. "You must not trust us," her parents would lament, "and you don't know what's best for your cousins. Let the adults handle it!"

After college, Kaitlyn ended up marrying a very wealthy and successful businessman who took care of her every need. As a rescuer, he stepped in and paid off her college loans and when a colleague at work gossiped about Kaitlyn, her husband called in some favors and found her a new position in the company far away from the gossip. Though Kaitlyn reveled in the protection and care she received from her doting husband, she sometimes felt that she couldn't handle her own problems, and that led her to panic and worry. What if something happened to her husband? Who would fight her battles for her? Kaitlyn also suffered from low self-esteem, believing that she didn't have the confidence and internal strength to handle any adversity on her own.

Does this resonate with you? Are you the victim in your own life story? Or, are you the "savior" to the victim in the form of ...

ROLE #3: THE RESCUER

"I'm just a peacekeeper. All I do is take care of everyone. I never say how *I* feel about anything. I just do whatever people want me to do because I don't want to cause trouble."

These are just a few of the words you may hear from the mouth of a rescuer. Rescuers are typically people who sponge, or absorb others' feelings and then they take on the feelings themselves. Not only that, rescuers believe they are responsible for making things right for others by making them feel better and solving their problems. They want to help and they want to take the other person's pain away. They think, "I can solve this problem. I can do it!"

Rescuers usually feel they:

- Can solve others' problems
- Must take on others' pain and make it go away
- Are responsible for other people's feelings
- Don't have a voice when it comes to what they personally want and need, and
- Shouldn't express their needs.

Stereotypical of parents who are rescuers is that they are always wanting to save the day for their children—advocating for what they think they need, especially when it comes to any activities or events where there is training, coaching or competition involved.

Or, consider the parent who stays home with the children—but spends so much of each day taking care of the kids that he or she begins to feel unappreciated and frustrated that there is no time for self-care. Or maybe it's the spouse who feels pressured to be the breadwinner because their partner can't seem to hold down a job. No matter the circumstances, the key feeling or component of a rescuer role is the need to help others to an unhealthy degree to the exclusion of his or her own needs. Unlike a victim, the rescuer has a strong sense of efficacy when it comes to helping others. And ironically, the rescuer wishes someone would take care of him or her every once in a while. However, this person will reject offers from others for help. That's because if others do help, then what would be the role of the rescuer? Not surprisingly, feelings of resentment and self-pity are common among rescuers. Left unchecked, these negative feelings can lead to dysfunctional relationships.

THE DANCE OF DRAMA: WHEN WE SWITCH ROLES

Remember, even if you identify with one role more closely than others, it is likely that at certain points in your life and under specific circumstances, you may shift into other roles. This role reversal tends to happen quickly and many times people aren't even consciously aware they are doing it. Look at how easily this happens:

Once, my stepmother was complaining about my dad: "I am really upset, Randee, because he's just sitting around, watching TV and gaining weight. He's not paying any attention to me." Clearly, my stepmother was the victim while my dad was the perpetrator.

But when she asked me to talk to him, the roles quickly changed.

I talked to him, trying to explain my stepmother's side of things. At this point, I was the rescuer. But the conversation quickly disintegrated because my father wanted to hear nothing of it. He started yelling, "This is none of your business! How dare you!" He was accusing me of meddling—in other words, being a perpetrator—yet, ironically when he started yelling at me I quickly morphed from rescuer to perpetrator and back to victim. Within ten minutes, I had experienced all three roles without even realizing it at the time.

So, how can you break the cycle, especially if it's been ingrained in you over the course of many years? First, notice when you're falling into these roles. Basically, any feeling that bothers you—and you don't know why it's agitating, irritating, angering or frustrating you so much—is a clue that you're operating within a role. In other words, your reaction is disproportionate to the actual situation. If you were upset because someone wouldn't give you a one-dollar refund and you then blew up at the customer service rep in response, this overreaction could be the result of a role you're falling into that dates back to your childhood.

Simply being aware of your role is vital: your conscious awareness is the first step in realizing that you need to change. Then, as you get more adept at pinpointing times and places in which you are most susceptible to these roles, you can use the "I" statements (discussed in greater detail in the next chapter) to express your feelings in a healthier way. By substituting the "I" statement for your typical reaction, you will subvert your need to become a perpetrator, rescuer or victim—and instead learn how to just be *you*—a person with needs and wants, asking others to take your *feelings* into account.

Here's an example: Jude is upset with his wife, Sharon, because she constantly criticizes the way he does the laundry. Instead of being valued for pitching in around the house, he feels that his gesture of goodwill is met with nagging.

Normally in these situations, Jude (the victim), seeks an escape by leaving the house to meet up with friends or go for a run. But this time, Jude realizes he's fallen into the victim role—while his wife is the perpetrator. Instead of running away, he tries an "I" statement:

Jude: "Honey, I feel belittled when I'm told I do the laundry the wrong way."

Sharon: "Belittled? I'm just trying to show you how to fold the shirts so they don't wrinkle."

Jude: "Yes, I get that, but when I'm constantly told it's wrong, it makes me feel frustrated and diminished."

Sharon: "Jude, I'm sorry! That was never my intention."

Even if it's difficult right now for you to believe that something as simple as an "I" statement could result in an apology (like Sarah's from above), I promise you that it's very difficult for the other person to continue to attack when you're not a willing participant. When you first try this, you might not receive an apology right away—but you will at least get the other person's attention by refusing to fall into old patterns. And over time, with patience and practice, you stand an excellent chance of positive receptivity from your partner, because your enhanced communication skills are contagious!

This may sound overly simplistic, but it's surprising how easily we fall into roles, unaware that it's happening. By becoming aware and employing the "I" statement strategy, you will find that a profound shift occurs. Rather than feeling the need to be right (perpetrator), to find a savior (rescuer) or get someone else to fight your battles (victim), you will be empowered to communicate positively with others. In return, you will begin to notice that the other person can't play the role if you're not willing to engage in the negative drama.

WHEN ONE PERSON IN THE SYSTEM CHANGES, IT ELICITS A CHANGE IN THE WHOLE SYSTEM.

Always remember that the way out of an emotional triangle is to practice one-on-one communication only. Two people, not three! Your communication needs to consist of *respect, consistency* and *honesty*. Recognize too that honesty without sensitivity is brutality and being brutally honest will only add fuel to the fire. As you practice speaking in a one-on-one dyad your family members, friends, coworkers and others will come to trust you more and more.

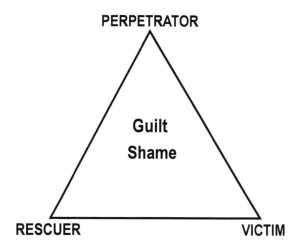

PERPETRATOR

Guilt
Shame

RESCUER   VICTIM

**The way out of the Triangle is
using "I Statements"
AND
ONE ON ONE COMMUNICATION
which consists of**

Honesty
Respect **= TRUST**
Consistency

EXERCISE: TRACKING AWARENESS AND SETTING THE STAGE FOR CHANGE

For the next week, here's your assignment: identify five times when you realize you're sinking into an old role. Remember, you are most likely reverting to a role if you:

- Become judgmental, rude, critical, accusatory or angry (this is the role of the perpetrator)
- Feel helpless, hopeless and incapable of taking care of yourself (this is the role of a victim)
- Try to step in and "save" someone or solve someone else's problems (this is the role of the rescuer)

When this week did you notice you were playing a role?

1. _____

2. _____

3. _____

4. _____

5. _____

Next, for each of the roles identified above, tune into the feelings you are experiencing and translate those emotions in the form of an "I" statement. For example:

- "I'm feeling irritated because I don't like this change in our family routine."
- "I feel sad because I was really looking forward to going to the movies."
- "I feel frustrated because I don't like to see other people suffering."

For each instance you identified above where you were playing a role, create an "I" statement:

1. _____

2. _____

3. _____

4. _____

5. _____

For added impact, journal details of your experiences.

Chapter 3

The Power of "I"(or The I's Have It)

"When you give yourself permission to communicate what matters to you in every situation you will have peace despite rejection or disapproval. Putting a voice to your soul helps you to let go of the negative energy of fear and regret."

- Shannon L. Alder

Sandy, a young woman in her twenties would boast to me about her honesty with others. When she initially began seeing me for sessions, she was very impressed with the fact that she felt comfortable telling people how she felt, what she thought and what others should be doing. For example, she might tell her boyfriend, "You're so thoughtless. You always forget my birthday!" And to a girlfriend she might note, "You really should break up with that loser. You can do so much better!" With colleagues, she would frequently advise, "All of you should stop being so sensitive when the boss gives you some constructive criticism!"

Not surprisingly, those around her didn't always react favorably to this advice, yet she was confused. *Why is everyone so mean? Why do they act so intimidated around me?* Sandy wondered. She couldn't understand what was happening because, in her mind, she was simply being up-front with everyone.

Unfortunately, this brand of honesty comes at a cost. Without intending to, Sandy was hurting people's feelings with her insensitive comments and ideas. Though she perceived it to be healthy to express herself, she was actually trying to control others with her brutal words. Honesty without sensitivity is brutality.

Over time, she realized that her need to stand up for herself stemmed from a lack of parental guidance in her youth. Sandy's mother died when she was young and her father wasn't very active in his daughter's life. Without the involvement that she craved from her parents, Sandy used her harsh honesty as a way of justifying herself and her existence to others.

Not only that, she was actually repeating her parents' communication styles. When her mother was still living, both parents lacked sensitivity in their interactions with their daughter—all in the name of honesty. Speeches and lectures would invariably begin with: "You never … ," "You always … ," and, "When will you learn how to … ?" Basically, her parents were shaming her with honesty, so when she turned around as an adult and would follow those same patterns … boom! She unintentionally shamed those around her.

She is not alone. Many of us, like Sandy, use our words, actions and expectations to guilt, shame or control others—whether or not we realize what we are doing. Notice that Sandy and her parents used one word, over and over—*you.* The word "you" can be used to blame and condemn others, and in this situation, that's exactly how the word was employed. When you start a conversation with the word "you," you are setting the other person up to be defensive.

A WINNING COMBINATION

Obviously, Sandy's friends and family did not enjoy her form of communication since positive communication demands more than just honesty. I like to think of it as an equation (as explained in chapter 2):

Honesty + Respect + Consistency = Positive Communication = Trust

In essence, share your thoughts in an honest and respectful manner, and if you consistently interact in this way, then positive rapport and interactions with others is practically guaranteed. The ones you love learn to trust you. Unfortunately, if you remove or minimize just one element of the equation, then your relationships will suffer. This was the case with Sandy: while she was certainly honest—and consistent in making those honest comments—there was nothing respectful in what she was saying or how she was saying it. Hence, the people in her life were not appreciative of her insights and opinions; instead they were turned off, resentful and diminished.

Sandy used a technique that allowed her to turn around her communication style and ultimately transform her relationships. Once Sandy learned to routinely use the technique I am about to teach you, she found that she could still be authentic with others, but in a much more loving, compassionate way. Not only did people begin to trust her, but they also felt that they could communicate with Sandy without fear of ridicule or rebuke.

The Power of "I"

"I" STATEMENTS

When you interact with others, in order for your communication to be clear and well received, it is essential to stop the following dysfunctional habits and behaviors:

- Blaming others
- "Should-ing" (telling people what they "should" think, do, believe, etc.) and
- Ridiculing (with put-downs, sarcasm, etc.).

Behaviors like these become habitual over time, and we aren't even always aware that we are blaming and shaming. Habits are hard to change at the best of times. So, how much more difficult is it to change when it's a bad habit, or we're not even aware that we are doing it? The reality is it's not that difficult to change, as long as you know *what* to do differently, *how* to do it differently and then—most importantly—you actually *do* things differently!

It is highly likely that you will feel a little awkward or maybe even feel a bit uncomfortable at first, but I promise you that using "I" statements is an incredibly easy technique to learn. Actually this uses less emotion and energy once you become comfortable with it.

ANATOMY OF AN "I"

First, let's look at what constitutes a healthy, positive "I" statement. These statements:

- *Do not* have the word "you" in them.
- Describe how you *feel*.
- Are used in response to how you feel when someone does or says something that triggers you or affects you. (Note: You will know you are being triggered because you may become angry, defensive or upset—and the intensity of those feelings will probably be disproportionate to the actual comment or action from the other person.)

Here's an example: Barbara was rushing around all day, trying to clean the house, get the kids fed, finish her own work from the office and get herself showered and ready for a much-needed date night with her husband, Ted. She had been looking forward to this night all week, and she wanted to have everything in order on the home front so she could truly relax at their favorite restaurant. But when she wasn't quite ready to leave for their 8 o'clock reservation, Ted offhandedly commented, "Late again?"

That's all it took for Barbara to go ballistic. She started screaming at Ted, "What do you think I've been doing all day? While you're watching the football game, I've been doing the laundry, taking care of the kids and running errands … not to mention doing my own work! And what about you? You never help out around the house! All you do is take, take, take …"

And with that, Barbara and Ted's romantic date night was effectively over.

What happened? Was Barbara off base? Maybe not; maybe Ted really was taking advantage of Barbara. Or, maybe she *was* overreacting. Perhaps Ted normally helped out, but after an unusually busy week, he decided to kick back and relax for a few hours. Regardless of the circumstances leading up to this event—and regardless of who's "right" or "wrong"—it is clear that Barbara had been triggered, since her reaction to Ted's seemingly innocuous comment activated an extremely angry response.

Of course, you're not Barbara. You're not living her life, so it's easy to observe this scenario and easily understand that her reaction was not likely to end well for either one of them. Yet how often do we do the same thing in our lives? One misstep from a spouse, parent, friend or child and we're yelling and screaming. And once we get started, it's easy to lose perspective and blame, dredge up the past and try to make the other person feel as badly as we do. It's also easy to fire back with lots of accusatory "you" statements, similar to what Barbara did.

That's why it's critical that, instead of lashing out when you feel emotions like pain or disappointment that you take time to experience what you are feeling and then clearly express those emotions rather than responding with anger and accusations. Are you feeling sad? Anxious? Worried? Agitated? Frustrated? Disappointed?

In Barbara's situation, she could have moved beyond the initial anger to tap into what she was really feeling and then shared something like, "I feel frustrated and misunderstood when no one acknowledges the work I do around the house." Expressing how she felt—as opposed to accusing Ted of being clueless—removes the blame—and therefore eliminates Ted's need to defend himself. The same applies to your relationships: if you keep the focus on your personal feelings through the "I" statement, the other party can truly focus on *you*. And that's when authentic, productive communication begins.

Another important reason to use "I" statements is because they help you own and be responsible for your own feelings. For instance, your husband has been ignoring you for a while. You finally explode and say "You've been ignoring me for days!" Then he says, "No I haven't, I spoke to you for twenty minutes yesterday." The healthy communication is "I am feeling neglected." Your husband cannot say "No you aren't" because that is YOUR feeling.

But before we go any further, let's practice noticing those feelings. First, get comfortable, and be still. Close your eyes, notice what you're feeling and say to yourself, "I feel happy. I feel sad. I feel agitated." Continue with other "feeling" statements, and note the emotion each statement evokes. Notice which part of your body feels the emotions most strongly.

For example, when I experience strong emotions I feel them in my stomach. It's as if a big wave of discomfort is washing over me. When I notice that feeling, I know it's time for an "I" statement.

Where do you feel your strong emotions in your body? Remember this because as you apply this exercise in the real world, I ask that you remain consciously aware of those feelings. In the times that you are feeling triggered, the "I" statements will help you honor the feelings and move them to a better place, energetically speaking. However, if you fail to honor those feelings, they will fester and eventually those emotions will bubble to the surface—and may manifest themselves as physical complaints, overreactions to others, etc.

EXERCISE: CRAFTING YOUR OWN "I" STATEMENTS

Now that you are getting in touch with your true feelings, it's time to link those emotions to a real situation. Think back to a time when you became angry and lashed out at a partner, spouse or friend. What led up to the outburst? What did the other person say or do? What did you say or do in response?

The first thing to do is consider how you were really *feeling*. In the heat of the moment, it's easy to think we are feeling an emotion when we react in anger, but anger isn't a true emotion. It is a behavior. There is always a primary feeling before the anger and that is either hurt or fear accompanied by issues such as feeling abandoned, disappointed, neglected, unsupported, annoyed or devastated. What was the feeling you had just before you moved it to anger?

Once you've identified the feeling, transform it into an "I" statement. Here are some examples:

- I feel hurt when I hear that tone of voice.
- I feel uncomfortable in that type of situation.
- I feel dismissed when I'm not validated for the contributions I make.
- I feel frustrated when I feel I'm not being heard or understood.
- I feel neglected when I don't get enough positive feedback.
- I feel diminished when I'm asked to account for my whereabouts.

- I feel overwhelmed when I have too many obligations all at once.
- I feel worried when I think we might be late.

It is not necessary for me to list "I" statements for all the possible feelings you can express. In my experience there are really only a few emotions that continue to be repeated in your relationships that are not being honored or dealt with. I am simply including examples that I have noticed are the most frequent ones in my practice.

Notice how not one of those examples has the word "you" in it.

It does take practice to use "I" statements without the word "you." My advice to you is this: in the beginning take time to pause before you speak as without conscious effort you will naturally revert to habitual patterns of the past. When you start using them in real conversations, you have to resist the inclination to make it about the other person and resist blaming them with "you" statements because it's not about them, it's about you and how you're feeling. Using "I" statements will not only make you more aware of yourself and where your feelings are coming from but it also frames the conversation in a way that the other person is practically forced to honor your feelings; you've removed blame from the equation and moved the focus away from the other person and onto *yourself*.

In addition to negative feelings, you can focus on positive feelings, too—especially if you're not used to sharing them with the important people in your life. Not only does this make others feel good, but it also helps you to put things into perspective. Here are some examples of "statement starters" for the positives in your life:

- I feel happy ...
- I feel supported ...
- I feel grateful ...
- I feel at peace ...

When you begin to use "I" statements, you will naturally begin to reframe the words you say. You're expressing your feelings and needs in a more compassionate manner rather than ignoring them. In fact, "I" statements help you follow the honesty/respect/consistency equation for positive communication with others. Additionally, when you communicate like this, trust is established.

The more you own your feelings and express them, the more clarity you will infuse into your relationships, and this can be both energizing and empowering for you and for others. By removing the need for the other person to feel defensive, you'll find that others will increasingly support of the way you feel. This will lead to a sense of strength and inner peace that you may have never felt before. For many people, using "I" statements is the first time they begin to feel validated by others for having (and expressing) their true feelings.

ALWAYS REMEMBER: AN "I" STATEMENT A DAY KEEPS THE CONFLICT AWAY!

Hint: Start practicing with innocuous everyday situations, since highly charged scenarios may make it difficult for you to reframe your reactions and feelings into an effective "I" statement. Once you become adept at using "I" statements, then you can begin moving into the more emotionally charged territories in your life.

Here is a simple template you can use to help you create "I" statements:

I feel _____(indicate your emotion) when _____
(give situation).

You may find yourself realizing where you could have used an "I" statement but didn't. You can always go back to the person and say: "I felt _____(indicate your emotion) when_____ happened (give situation)."

If you have difficulty identifying your feelings please Google "a list of emotions." You will be surprised at how many feelings you have already felt but just didn't have the words to describe.

Practice this exercise with your spouse or friend on a daily basis. Put ten minutes on the clock and practice making "I" statements to each other every day for a week.

Chapter 4
The Three-Sentence Rule

"The way we communicate with others and with ourselves ultimately determines the quality of our lives"

- Tony Robbins

Jonathan's mother Pauline, is visiting for the weekend. Unfortunately, Jonathan's wife Samantha isn't too excited. That's because every time Pauline visits, she spends the majority of her time criticizing Samantha. Worst of all, Jonathan not only ignores his mother's negative commentary, but also lets her order him around like a lap dog!

This particular weekend, Pauline was in rare form: after telling Samantha that the roast was so well-done it tasted like shoe leather, she proceeded to follow her daughter-in-law around the house, pointing out the stain on the carpet, the crooked picture on the wall and the large laundry pile.

Pauline shook her head. "I just don't know how Jonathan lives like this! You know, my house always was—and always will be—immaculate!" Then she turned to Samantha and wagged her finger. "Dear, I worry if you keep this up, what's to stop your husband from looking around for someone who can really take care of him?"

After that comment, Samantha spent the remainder of the weekend holed up in the bedroom. When Jonathan tried to talk her into coming downstairs, Samantha snapped. "Just go find yourself someone more acceptable to your mother, Jonathan! That's what you want anyway, isn't it?"

But the more Jonathan tried to console her, the angrier Samantha became, until she finally grabbed her purse and stormed out of the house.

"Where are you going?" Jonathan yelled as Samantha opened the door of her car.

"Anywhere but here!" And with that, Samantha slammed the car door and sped away, the tires squealing.

In this situation, Samantha is clearly the target of Pauline's bullying, and her husband was doing little to defend his wife from his mother's barbed comments. Though he knew the two of them never got along, Jonathan was reluctant to create a stir with his mother, so he normally tried to keep the peace between the two women. And because Samantha usually kept her feelings to herself when it came to her mother-in-law, Jonathan wrongly assumed the situation was tolerable. To be fair, Jonathan rarely heard the most nasty of comments from Pauline, as she was smart enough to save her vitriol for times she and Samantha were alone. Jonathan had no clue that Pauline had done or said anything wrong that weekend; he was busy washing his car and catching up on paperwork most of the day, so he wasn't even within earshot of the criticisms and passive-aggressive behaviors.

Obviously this couple's "process timing" is off, which I'll talk more about in Chapter Six. However, I would suggest that once they become adept at adjusting their process timing to state their feelings (through "I" statements) and validating one another, they would be ready to move on to *The Three-Sentence Rule.*

The beauty of the Three-Sentence Rule is that you simply speak in three brief statements:

1. Explain the situation.
2. Share your feeling.
3. Tell what you need.

This process is basically an expansion of "I" statements. It is designed for people who tend to be more naturally verbal as it allows them to express themselves more easily and with greater clarity. For those that are not naturally verbal, it provides a good structure for communication.

When you explain the situation, describe what has happened that is causing conflict. At this stage, it is OK to say "you," because you are trying to convey to your partner what he or she did that upset you. For example, "When we were at that party, you said that you couldn't stand my friends." Essentially, you are setting the scene for what was happening and this will allow you to describe how these circumstances made you feel. The partner who is hearing the word "you" must do his or her best not to get offended or defensive, because you are not going to attack him or her. Instead, after explaining the situation, you are going to say, "This is how I felt, and this is what I needed." For example: "I felt hurt and judged in regards to who my friends are and I need my friends to be accepted."

The Three-Sentence Rule is a terrific way to stop the "long talk." There are people who tell me they were arguing and fighting for two hours the night before they see me. Certainly, talking, discussing and fighting fair are fine—but it should never, ever take hours. There is absolutely no need for that.

For Samantha and Jonathan, Samantha might say the following to Jonathan: "When your mom visits she criticizes me when you are not present. I feel hurt and judged. I need you to be with me when she is around."

Note that Samantha never shifts the blame to Jonathan; even though he might be to blame for being so clueless, at this point the main issue is with Pauline. With the Three-Sentence Rule, Samantha makes it clear what has been happening, how she feels about it and how Jonathan can help her. And because Jonathan truly wants to improve the situation, he now knows exactly how he can remedy it!

The Three-Sentence rule makes conversations direct, clear, straight and honest; because if you have to keep going back and forth, hour after hour, no one is getting validated and no one is being heard.

The exercise below will walk you through the Three-Sentence Rule step by step:

3 Sentence Rule

1. Explain the SITUATION

2. Share your FEELING

3. Tell what you NEED

EXERCISE: THE THREE-SENTENCE RULE

1. Think back to a time when you were upset with your partner's behavior.
2. Condense the entire situation into one sentence that describes what happened. For example, "Last night when I started to tell you about my day, you turned away from me and started texting on your phone."
3. Think about how you felt about what happened and turn that into an "I" statement. For example: "When that happened, I felt neglected and diminished."
4. Express what you needed to feel better in that situation: "I needed you to look at me and really listen to what I was saying without the distraction of your phone."

If you have trouble remembering it all, write down your three statements before sharing with your partner. With time and practice, the three statements will be easy for you to formulate, and you won't need to write them down any more.

Best of all, you can use this strategy in positive situations, too: "When we were at the party, you knew I was uncomfortable and feeling left out, so I felt so excited and supported when you stayed by my side the entire time. Could you do this for me with more consistency?"

The brevity of these statements makes it easy for your partner to hear what you're saying and really process your words quickly and seamlessly. Furthermore, you prevent lengthy arguments by "editing" the circumstances into a single statement, and then turning to your feelings and needs immediately. Instead of feeling attacked, your partner will instantly understand why you were so upset. You're also providing a solution, so that he or she knows what could have been done (and what can be done in the future) to improve the situation.

This is one of my favorite and most powerful strategies, because it harnesses the power of the "I" statements while setting the stage for your partner to validate your feelings and needs quickly and easily. Try it during your nightly sessions and see for yourself how this rule can improve your relationships!

Chapter 5
Validate Me, Please!

"You cannot truly listen to anyone and do anything else at the same time."

- M. Scott Peck

Vera slips into the new dress she bought for a girls' night out. As she zips up the dress she notices how it pulls around her waist. "Dave!" she complains to her husband. "I must be gaining weight! Look how fat I am in this dress. I can just imagine the comments Ashley will make ... "

Dave glances at Vera and says, "Honey, I think you look amazing! And don't worry so much about Ashley; she's your friend. She shouldn't be judging you ... "

Vera shakes her head as the tears fill her eyes. He just doesn't get it!

Meanwhile, Dave is thinking: Why are my comments upsetting her? I'm only trying to build her up and have her not worry so much about what others think!

The situation above is all too common: one partner is upset and shares those feelings. The other person, meanwhile, tries to either fix the problem or explain it away—and then wonders why his or her partner doesn't appreciate the compliments and well-meaning advice.

Even when the partner's intentions are pure, the reason these typical communications break down so quickly is that they are lacking one critical ingredient:

Validation.

You see, validation isn't about understanding *why* your friend, partner, colleague, etc. feels a certain way. Rather, it is simply understanding that your partner actually feels certain feelings and those feelings need to be acknowledged. Validation does not mean that you're "faking" agreement, or that you agree or disagree with what the person is saying. It is the recognition that those feelings are *real* for him or her.

No matter the situation, validating someone's feelings lets them know that they have been heard and acknowledged at a very deep level; it allows that person to move on. But when feelings are not validated, they continue to get more and more frustrated, and in the heat of the moment this can lead to crying, yelling, slammed doors, and other unwanted behaviors. Think back to Vera. Her behaviors aren't a result of her wanting to be five years old again; it's simply that she's trying to be heard, understood and acknowledged by Dave. The dysfunctional behaviors never achieve the intended objective, but (like Vera) so many of us continue the insanity until we feel sure that our voices are heard. Unfortunately, until Vera begins to feel validated by Dave, no amount of advice or problem-solving on his part will improve the situation.

When you hear a person repeat themselves over and over again, that is a signal that they don't feel heard or validated. Remember that you don't have to agree or disagree, just acknowledge that what they are feeling is real for them.

The trick is to not get stuck in the content or tone of what is being said. Instead, simply acknowledge that this person does, in fact, feel angry, sad, upset, diminished, etc. One other caveat: when validating someone, please don't take it personally. Realize that it's about the other person's feelings—not you. Even if your wife says, "I feel ignored in the evenings" and you know that you've tried to spend time with her after work, know that it really isn't about you. It's about how she feels. If, however, you take it personally, you will not be able to separate yourself from the feelings and the other person's feelings will remain validated.

Validation makes it a safe environment to share feelings within your relationships. It's difficult to communicate your feelings if you don't think the other person is going to hear you—or, worse yet, if the other person is likely to criticize you for those feelings.

So, what could Dave have done differently to elicit a more positive reaction? A simple, "I'm sorry you're feeling so blue—that must be stressful to feel that way," could de-escalate Vera's feelings. Notice that Dave is not agreeing that Vera is "fat"—or that Ashley is going to trash talk behind Vera's back. Instead, he's simply empathizing with her, which lets Vera know that Dave is listening and understands how upset she feels.

**There is No Right or Wrong
Just Acknowlege Others Feelings...**

**This Creates a Safe Environment
to Share Feelings**

EXERCISE: CRACKING THE VALIDATION CODE, PART ONE

Unlike "I" statements, when validating someone, it is OK to use the word "you." You will find that it is nearly impossible to truly validate another person without it! Check out these validating statements:

- That must have been so annoying for you.
- I get that this was very frustrating.
- You must have really felt awful that your feelings were hurt.
- You must feel so bothered and upset!
- It sounds like you are so happy.

Easy, right? Simply *hear* what the other person is saying ... and then translate that feeling into a validating statement. A validating statement follows the other person's "I" statement. However, so that you don't sound like a parrot, avoid repeating the exact same words back to your partner. Instead, find a synonym for the emotion and use that word instead. When you validate it is best not to say "I understand." No one can really understand what another is feeling.

EXERCISE: CRACKING THE VALIDATION CODE, PART TWO

In the second part of this exercise, I'm going to ask you to practice validating a friend, partner, spouse, or colleague. Choose someone to work with who is willing to make an "I" statement that you can follow up with a validation. It's important to role-play validating others first, because this can be a difficult skill to master in the heat of a real argument or emotional conversation.

Once you find your practice partner, brainstorm situations in which the other person tends to get agitated, upset or frustrated. Then, ask your partner to make an "I" statement that describes his/her feelings. Your job is to follow up with a validating statement. After you get used to validating the other person, switch roles. Now you make the "I" statement while the other person validates you.

Notice how positive the communication becomes and how empowering it is to be heard and understood. Here are a few sample statements to help you along:

- *Janie:* The anniversary of my mother's death is coming up soon and I feel so sad.
- Validator: I'm so sorry you're feeling unhappy; that must be upsetting for you.
- *Jim:* I feel incompetent when I am constantly reminded to take out the trash.
- *Validator:* I get it. It must be very uncomfortable to continually feel nagged.

Barb: I feel so frustrated because I have mentioned places I would like to go that are important to me, but we still haven't gone.

- *Validator:* It sounds like you are irritated that you keep repeating yourself and don't feel that you're getting cooperation.

One final hint: Once you've been validated, be sure to say, "thank you" to the other person. However, if you *don't* feel validated, don't lie! Simply follow-up with, "I need that reworded, please." Or, you can even use an "I" statement such as, "I don't feel validated." Then the validator tries a different statement. This allows the validator to ensure that the other person truly feels satisfied that he or she has been heard.

People who come from families that did not acknowledge or discuss feelings may have difficulty picking a synonym for the others person's feelings. Please Google a list of feeling words and have them with you while doing the validating. If you have difficulty finding lists of feelings, please visit my website at www. DrRandee.com.

You can even teach this to children by being role models of good communication. Share what you did today at work, and use "I" statements to express your feelings; then, your partner can respond by validating your feelings. Eventually, your children will learn that they can feel safe expressing their emotions, since their parents demonstrate how to have conversations about how they really feel!

BONUS TIP: BREAKING THE CYCLE WITH "I" STATEMENTS AND VALIDATION

When a person is angry and they are yelling at another person, it is usually a tip-off that they do not feel validated. Most likely, what is really happening is that the person has tried to explain to how he or she felt, but their loved one might not have "gotten it." If this has happened to you, at the time you probably thought the person just wanted to start an argument—but in reality, he or she just wanted to be heard.

As mentioned in Chapter Two, when people don't receive the validation they need, they often fall back into their roles of the Karpman Triangle.[2] If, say, I thought my husband should pay more attention to me—since he hadn't spent time with me in the past three days—I might walk up to him and say, "You've been ignoring me for three days."

This is hardly the kind of approach that would result in him being apologetic and with an overwhelming desire to change his ways. In this situation, I'm the perpetrator and my husband's the victim, so he's going to try to defend himself. Or, if he's tired of accusations, he may even turn the tables and accuse *me* of being inaccurate: "No, I haven't been ignoring you! Just yesterday, I talked to you for twenty minutes." Notice that no one is getting his or her needs met, and the "you" statements are just escalating the conflict.

However, if I simply used an "I" statement, I could begin to find my way out of the triangle. For example, I could say, "Honey, I've been feeling neglected for the past three days." At this point, I haven't accused my husband of anything, so he won't feel attacked. And, because my words have not put him on the defensive, he's not going to argue with my statement. In this scenario it would be difficult to argue with how I feel, because if I say, "I feel neglected," he can't—in all truthfulness—say "No you don't." The feelings

---

2   Karpman, S. (n.d.). The Official Site of the Karpman Drama Triangle. Retrieved October 3, 2015, from http://www.karpmandramatriangle.com

are mine to own and simply sharing them with him allows him to understand what is going on with me.

As you can see, validation is an important concept. It acknowledges another person's feelings. It's a way to let someone know that you recognize what he or she is feeling is *real* for him/her. Once you understand how easy it is to put into practice, you'll find it to be an invaluable communication tool.

Chapter 6
Timing Is Everything

"You don't have to swing hard to hit a home run. If you got the timing, it'll go."

- Yogi Berra

It's 10:00 p.m. on a Thursday evening. Marcia is sitting alone at the kitchen table. There is a plate of food across from her, but her plate is empty. She takes one last look at her watch and stands up. As she scrapes steak from the full plate into the dog's bowl, her husband enters the room.

David: *"I'm home! What's for dinner?"*

Marcia: *"Dinner was hours ago. Why didn't you call to say you're going to be late—again?"*

David (confused): *"Why, what's the problem?"*

Marcia (annoyed): *"It's ten o'clock, and dinner was at eight!"*

David (clueless): *"No problem, I just got delayed a bit at the bar. But I'm here now."*

[David pours a glass of wine for Marcia, hands it to her and puts his arms around her.]

Marcia (still annoyed): *"It's too late now."*

David (still clueless): "Why?"
Marcia (exasperated): "Because I'm not cooking at this hour."
David (whining): "But all my friends' wives cook at this time ... "
Marcia (glaring): "I don't understand why you are so upset."
David (hurt): "Why are you being so mean to me?"

No, this isn't a script from a play; it's actually a true interaction between two of my clients. David can't understand why Marcia's so upset, and Marcia can't believe that David is being so thoughtless about an issue they've discussed many times before.

Arguments such as these are all too common for couples, and though the circumstances vary, there is one thing that most miscommunication has in common: the partners' *process timing* is off.

Process Timing is the order in which you naturally process infor-mation. We all think, feel and behave. Everyone does all three but what you do may be in a different order to that of your partner. Thoughts are simply all of the ideas that are in your head; this is the intellectual modality. A feeling, on the other hand, is what you feel somewhere in your body; and some people may feel it in their head, stomach or heart. Basically, feeling is an emotion. And behavior is the action (or non-action) that you take. Behaviors include actions like shutting down, storming out or talking without filters. Many of the behaviors exhibited during a conflict are quite reactive and passive-aggressive. The most important part of process timing is the recognition that what you do third is what you do least.

Even though you and your partner cycle through all three of these modalities in your interactions, it's quite likely that the order is different. While you might think, feel and then behave, your partner might behave first, think second and feel last.

When couples experience conflict, it's often because their *process timing* is in sync: they are processing things in a different order to their partner's. For example, David tends to behave before thinking or feeling. His *process timing* would be behave—think—feel. Meanwhile, Marcia feels first, then behaves and thinks last; Marcia's process timing is feel—behave—think.

David	Marcia
Behave	Feel
Think	Behave
Feel	Think

David *behaves* the moment he walks through the door. He expects his wife to provide dinner for him, even at this late hour, without even thinking about how his wife must feel. Marcia, however, is *feeling* upset that he is so late and annoyed that he didn't call. Marcia voices her frustrations, but since David is not yet *feeling*, he is oblivious to how Marcia *feels* in this moment. Because David does not acknowledge her feelings, Marcia *behaves*, refusing to cook dinner. With this behavior, David begins to *think*, "why, what's the problem?" He doesn't understand the cause or origin of this behavior, but is attempting to *think* through it. Since David still does not understand why Marcia is behaving this way, he begins to *feel* hurt that his wife won't make him dinner. Marcia, unaware of how he is feeling at this moment, tries to *think* about the nature of his actions, about why he is so upset about this situation.

Because Marcia and David operate on entirely different *process timing* schedules, neither one of them has their feelings validated by the other. Behaviors can then be misinterpreted or misunderstood, since neither Marcia nor David understands the reasoning behind them or the feelings that initiate them. Without any intervention, this offset of their *process timing* will create further tension and strife as they continue cycling through mismatched processes.

However, with knowledge of your different *process timings*, it is possible to adjust the cycles and allow for greater understanding of each other's feelings and behaviors. In counseling sessions, I will encourage someone like David to curb his natural tendency to *behave* first by suggesting that he *think* about the situation and get in touch with his feelings *before* speaking. I'll work with Marcia to prioritize her *think* stage, forcing her to understand more quickly why she *feels* a particular emotion and to allow her to express her opinions (*behave*) to David in a more productive manner. By slowing David down and accelerating Marcia's self-expression, it is easier for David to understand where Marcia is coming from. It's also advantageous for Marcia to not *behave* before understanding the source of her emotions. With these adjustments, the dialogue may sound something like this:

David: *"I'm home! What's for dinner?"*

Marcia: *"Dinner was hours ago. Why didn't you call to say you're going to be late—again?"*

David (*realizing that Marcia sounds upset, he attempts to learn more*): *"Honestly, I forgot to call. Are you OK?"*

Marcia (*thinking about the origin of her emotions and sending an "I" statement*): *"Actually, I'm not. When there's no one here to eat with me—especially after I spent an hour preparing dinner—I feel neglected."*

David (*validating*): *"I'm sorry you felt uncared for; that must have been upsetting to spend all that time cooking—only to eat alone."*

Marcia (*relieved*): *"Thank you for listening, David.*

With the adjustments to their *process timing*, Marcia and David are much more equipped to validate each other's feelings. Actually, if Marcia and David can be on think mode at the same time, a lot of this miscommunication will be reduced.

The best way to work on your *process timing* is to know your *own* personal tendencies. Once you've identified those, your partner can evaluate their predispositions and eventually you can work on synchronizing your timing as a couple.

A fun exercise to do with your partner is for each of you to guess each other's process timing. Ask each other what they think the other does first, second and third. Write your names next to each other and list your three modalities beneath so that they align and you can begin to see the possible causes of miscommunication.

Process Timing

EXERCISE: WHAT'S YOUR PROCESS TIMING?

This exercise allows you to tap into all three modalities (think, feel, behave) in order to identify your typical process timing. While you may have a preferred order it may vary depending on the situation and person with whom you're interacting.

1. Think back to a time where you were engaged in conflict with another person.
2. What did you do first? Following are possible scenarios that may resonate with you.:

BEHAVE: You immediately started talking, arguing, complaining, explaining your "side" of the situation, slamming doors or storming off, and so on.)

FEEL: You experienced many emotions bubbling to the surface; anger, disappointment, confusion, fear, sadness, tension, embarrassment, or a cascade of different feelings.

THINK: You logically thought through the situation; you rationalized and intellectualized.

3. Now, determine what you did next: Behave? Think? Feel?
4. Establish what you did last. For example, if you thought and behaved first and second, then feeling is your third modality.
5. Share your personal process timing with trusted friends and family. Are they in agreement with your perceptions? This is an important step because we

have so many personal biases that it may be difficult to objectively determine the order in which we think, feel and behave.

6. Finally, put it all together. Take your process timing and work to strengthen your third and weakest modality. You do this by being aware of the times when you're ready to operate from your first, preferred mode, and then simply hold off on that modality until you can cycle through the other two modes. For instance, if I tend to behave first, then the next time I realize I'm ready to go on a rant, I need to stop. In that pause, I'll think through the situation and tap into my feelings. By moving the other two modalities to the front, I am much more likely to act from a place of calm and thoughtfulness, rather than just lashing out and/or saying the first thing that pops into my head.

Once you've practiced this technique for a week or two, ask your partner to determine his or her own process timing as well. Once you're both aware of your own process timing—along with your partner's—you can help each other adjust your processes with signals.

Let's say your partner wants to work on curbing behavior (speaking) before thinking or feeling. For this, you can develop an agreed-upon signal so that the next time your partner is ready to spout off, you can give them the signal. In this way they allow themselves to become conscious of their own process and can choose to take the opportunity to do something different. The signal doesn't need to be complicated. It can be as simple as holding up two fingers, shaking your head "no" or holding your hand up with your palm out, as if to say "stop." If both of you agree to signal the other person, you can greatly accelerate your ability to alter your process timing and eventually you will be able to connect your timing with one another.

Remember, no one is perfect! Becoming consciously aware of what you're doing through the signal gives you both the chance for a do-over. By pausing before succumbing to your natural modality, you will respond to your partner in a much more compassionate way; and the more your partner feels respected and heard, the more positive your relationship becomes.

Chapter 7
Let Go of My Ego!

"Whenever I climb I am followed by a dog called 'Ego.'"

- Friedrich Nietzsche

Everyone has three ego states—Parent, Adult and Child—and we move through these states constantly, especially when we communicate with loved ones. While in the Parent ego state there are two subtypes of parent: Critical or Nurturing. In the Child ego state there are two subtypes: Rebellious or Complacent. The third ego state is the Adult and it considered the healthy one. These ego states are identifiable in our communication. When a person is in one of the ego states it sets the other partner up to be in the opposite ego state. For example, when someone is speaking like a critical parent they are setting the other up to be a rebellious child. And conversely when one is being a rebellious child they are setting the other up to be a critical parent. Many people are so comfortable with their roles from childhood that they continue to recreate these roles even in adulthood.

Consider the example below and determine who's acting like the "parent" and who's playing the role of the "child":

Melissa pulls into the driveway after a long day at work, noticing that Daniel did not put the trash out as he promised. Not only did he forget, but their already-overflowing trash cans won't be able to hold any new trash—and the truck won't be back for another week.

By the time Melissa reaches the front door, she's fuming. When she walks into the living room and finds Daniel asleep on the couch, she explodes: "Daniel, why didn't you take out the trash? You knew the cans were already full."

She continues her rant, and Daniel opens one eye as she's speaking. Knowing that she would never accept a simple "I forgot," Daniel invents a convoluted story about having terrible allergies that day, taking an antihistamine and then falling asleep before he could remember to take out the garbage.

Melissa halfheartedly listens to his explanations and then continues to vent and fume. At this point, Daniel has no intention of taking out the garbage—ever! If she's so concerned, Daniel thinks, she can take out the garbage herself.

In the example above, Melissa is acting like the critical parent. When she speaks to Daniel this way, it's going to trigger Daniel, and his knee-jerk reaction is to take on the role of the rebellious child. Their interaction is similar to the times when a parent says to a child, "Go to your room, young man, and do your homework!" Though the words and context are different, the tone of the communication is similar: Daniel is the naughty boy and Melissa is the demanding mother who is calling him on his faults and foibles. Daniel knows he should take the trash out but takes a nap instead. Knowing Melissa will get mad, he acts like a rebellious child by not taking the trash out, which is setting Melissa up to be a critical parent. Sadly, communications such as these are common in many partnerships and relationships.

Similarly, there are many couples that still behave like parents and children—except there is no nagging. Instead, one partner assumes the role of the "nurturing parent" and the other person plays the complementary role of the "complacent child." Take a look at how this plays out:

Miles is the epitome of a doting husband, doing whatever he can for his wife, Charlotte. He makes the dinner, washes the dishes and puts gas in her car when it needs it. Charlotte doesn't want to complain, because Miles acts so lovingly toward her, but she can't shake the feeling that he behaves more like a father than a husband. In fact, she almost feels an obligation to continually thank him for everything: "That was so nice of you, Miles! Thanks so much, dear … " and so on.

In this instance, Miles has confused loving with parental nurturing. While 'loving' is the adult expression of love, 'nurturing' is almost like babying the partner. This sets Charlotte up to be the complacent child. That too works in reverse. Charlotte sees that Miles has washed her car for her. She thanks him profusely for doing this and being so nice. This sets him up to be the nurturing parent.

Let go of my EGO

GETTING YOUR EGO FIX

In the examples above, there is one ego state that is missing in these dysfunctional communication patterns, and that is the Adult ego state. Without adult communication, other aspects of the relationship will suffer as well—and the couple's sex life often suffers the most. It's no surprise, since it's difficult to have intimacy in bed when one of you is the parent and the other is the child. It would be incestuous to have sex with your child, so in these imaginary roles you can't be fully mature, adult lovers.

Ego States

Parent	**Critical** **Nurturing**
Adult	**"I"**
Child	**Rebellious** **Complacent**

EXERCISE: WHAT ROLE DO YOU PLAY?

Carrying out this activity will bring greater awareness to the times and people with whom you've fallen into an unhealthy parent/child dynamic:

1. The Critical Parent Role: Think back to the times you played the part of the nagging, critical parent. What were your demands of the other person? How did he or she react?

2. The Nurturing Parent Role: Remember any time you felt the need to nurture and care for (rather than love) your partner. Hint: times you felt a need to protect the other person, or if you felt that he or she couldn't handle something alone (and that you needed to save the day).

3. The Rebellious Child Role: Now recall instances in which you were being criticized and reacted like a sullen, rebellious child. Maybe you purposely "forgot" or procrastinated, or maybe you feigned an inability to do what your partner was asking because you resented his or her demands.

4. The Complacent Child Role: Think back to any times when you felt compelled to comply with your partner because he or she was nurturing you into submission! You might have even had mixed feelings, knowing that the person was being very giving, caring, etc., while at the same time you felt helpless and immature because of their over-the-top nurturing.

5. If you can relate to any of the scenarios above, then in these situations you have moved away from a mature,

adult relationship and fallen back into roles that may have been comfortable as a child, but are unhealthy for a functional relationship now.

6. Take a week and observe your communication with someone close to you. Write down situations that you noticed where you assumed the ego states. The first step is being aware. Then share the situations with the person you are observing. Do a re-do by correcting how the communications could have been done in a healthy manner.

7. Sometimes the tone of voice from someone sounds more critical than what has been actually said. Share those instances as well.

To combat these unhealthy patterns, revisit Chapter Three to review the "I" statements. By using "I" statements, you can begin to connect more closely with your emotions, thereby diminishing your need to control (or be controlled by) the other person. The goal is to move into the adult role as quickly as you can. Whoever realizes first that they are in roles needs to take responsibility and make an "I" statement to encourage both to communicate adult to adult, husband to wife, lover to lover, etc.

The next time you become aware that one or both of you are playing these roles, express how you feel: "I am uncomfortable being spoken to that way," or "I feel resentful as if there's a critical parent talking to me." By shedding light on the dynamic, it draws attention to the pattern. And it is from that perspective that you and your partner can work toward restoring a healthier, adult form of communication and love.

Ch

Piles of Poop

"Unexpressed emotions will never die. They are buried alive and will come forth later in uglier ways."

- Sigmund Freud

When people are trying to communicate with each other and conflict arises, underneath it all there is always an original issue, feeling or concept. If that issue, feeling or concept is not validated or dealt with, a typical reaction for the person who feels invalidated or left unheard is to make a hurtful comment. Most likely, the recipient of the comment will then become defensive and fight back to protect his or her ego, reputation, etc. This dynamic sets a chain reaction in motion, where each person is triggering a reaction in the other. Eventually, there is no communication. There is only a reaction … to the reaction … to the reaction … to the reaction … and so on.

People who come to me for counseling often say, "Here, please fix this …" and they become immersed in all of the details about the other person's anger, nasty comments, temper, passive-aggressiveness,

...his, I immediately get out my whiteboard and begin
...f poop."

...t piles of poop. That's basically what's happening when
...ting entrenched in conflict with your partner. Something
...ong, and then you react, and then your partner reacts to you
...il pile after pile of dysfunction (the poop) begins to accumulate.
...ter a while, you no longer even remember what the original issue
was because you're so mired in poop!

In fact, many clients want me to deal with the fourth or fifth pile of poop. I won't go there because those piles are simply reactions that stemmed from the original issue. It is very important in all communications to acknowledge and honor the original issue, feeling or concept so that resulting reactions do not get out of control.

It is the nature of poor communication that most people aren't even aware that the poop is piling up—until it's too late. To illustrate this concept let's take a look at Harold and Kami, two friends who planned to meet for lunch at a restaurant:

Harold keeps looking at his watch, wondering what could've happened to Kami. He knows she typically runs late, but an hour and a half is a bit much! After two hours of trading impatient glares with the waiter, who wants nothing more than to clear his table for a couple who is actually eating (and tipping!), Harold picks up the phone and texts Kami. Within a minute, he receives a text back: "So sorry, Harold! Something came up, and I totally forgot to call. Let's reschedule next week, OK?"

Immediately, a host of emotions floods into Harold's awareness: he feels uncared for, disappointed and even unworthy that someone would ditch him! I'll show her, *Harold thinks as he shoves his phone into his pocket.* I'm not even texting her back.

Later that afternoon, Kami calls Harold. The first two times she calls, he let the phone switch over to voicemail. The third time, he picks up. "Hello?"

"Harold! Did you get my text and calls?"

Harold says tersely, "Yes, I got them."

Kami tries again. "OK, so, I am really sorry I flaked out like that! You'll never believe what happened ..." She then launches into a story and Harold barely listens.

"Uh-hmm," Harold replies as Kami finishes her story.

"Harold, are you upset with me?"

Harold feels a knot in his stomach but simply says, "I'm fine, Kami."

Kami sounds confused. "Harold, you don't sound fine. What's up?"

As the conversation continues, Kami tries to draw Harold out, but Harold has effectively shut her down and is now giving Kami his version of the silent treatment. Eventually, Kami prods and pushes so much that Harold feels obligated to tell her how he's feeling. But as he tells her, he wonders if he's risking their friendship by telling her how upset he is. He rationalizes that it's not that big a deal, and maybe he's making a mountain out of a molehill. At this point, he's feeling intense fear that he's jeopardizing the friendship.

Meanwhile, Kami is getting ticked off. Here she is, trying to apologize and find out if Harold is upset, but he's not being up-front with her.

In this example, can you see the layers of poop? We've got Harold shutting down, getting angry and feeling fearful. Then there's Kami, who is feeling overwhelmed, apologetic, confused and eventually angry. But what is at the core?

It all begins with Harold feeling uncared for because Kami stood him up. That's the original piece of poop! And that's what Harold needs to focus on—not the argument, the silent treatment or any other peripheral reaction.

Here is a visual example of how Harold and Kami get caught up in their piles of :

Piles of Poop

Reactions to Reactions

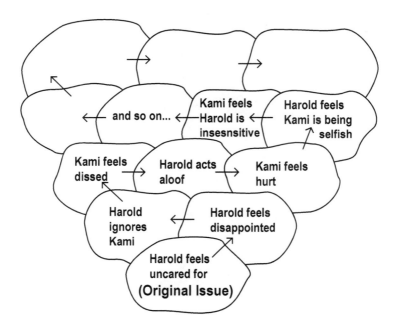

To really get to the root cause, you must first identify all of the reactionary piles of "poop." Then you need to clear them away and focus on the original issue.

It is the same thing when you think of your life. Consider all the times that you piled up the poop: all the occasions you reacted to another person, or they reacted to you, and the reactions continued to form layer upon layer until the original issue got covered up.

The danger of not addressing the original "poop" is that over time, we simply react, while ignoring the issue that lies deeper inside—the issue of which we are no longer aware. And when that original issue remains unresolved, you're likely to become extremely reactive without completely understanding why you're reacting so strongly.

To sift through the poop, so to speak, you need to ask yourself what is lurking beneath both you and your partner's reactions. Once you identify the core issues, you can begin to understand why you hurt so much.

EXERCISE: GETTING TO THE CORE

1. On a blank piece of paper, draw a diagram similar to the one above.

2. Think back to a time when someone upset you, let you down, where your feelings were hurt, etc. List that incident in the first piece of poop. This is the original issue.

3. Think back to your reaction to the experience, along with the other person's reactions. List all of those reactions in the other pieces of poop.

4. Continue listing each subsequent reaction until you have completely exhausted all of the reactions between you and your partner surrounding the original issue.

5. Now, cross out all the piles of poop—except for the original issue. You see, all of these other piles of poop really don't need to be stated or addressed, because they are not the problem—the original issue is.

6. Once you've identified the original issue, use "I" statements to explain what you were feeling. If necessary, revisit Chapter Three on "I" statements for a refresher regarding how to describe your feelings. Note: If your partner has not been joining you on all the exercises so far, you might need to ask them to (re-)read the chapter on validation in order to respond in a healthy way.

7. Switch roles. Have your partner draw his or her own piles of poop, following steps one through six. Now, it's your partner's turn to use "I" statements to express

their feelings with regards to their original issue. Again, be sure to validate your partner's statements to help properly address his or her core issue.

It is absolutely amazing how out of control the communication becomes without awareness of the original pile of poop. Remember: reaction is not communication, response to the original issue is. That's because whenever the conversation gets out of control, the original issue or feeling or concept has not been addressed and validated. However, with practice and consistency, you can keep the "poop" where it belongs … in the sewer.

Chapter 9

Past Pain and Future Fear: Give Yourself a Present!

"If you want to conquer the anxiety of life, live in the moment, live in the breath."

- Amit Ray

Lily was a happy, well-adjusted six-year-old with loving parents who took care of all her needs—until the day they rocked her young world with the news that they were getting a divorce. Now, she was going to live with her mother during the week and then spend time with her father on the weekends. Lily couldn't understand why this was happening. In her mind, everything had been just fine!

Lily never completely recovered from this traumatic event. Even as an adult, whenever she feels that things are going well for her, Lily fears there must be something lurking around the corner that will steal her joy.

Quite often, people who have been hurt get stuck between two difficult places: past pain and future fear. It is not uncommon to feel pain from the past, since most of us have experienced dysfunction at one time or another—whether it was from a difficult upbringing, a failed relationship, a death of a loved one or something else. It only becomes problematic when we can't get past the pain and become embedded in it is the fear of a doomed future. It's as if there's no way we could ever enjoy something positive. As the cliché goes, we are "waiting for the other shoe to drop."

Trusting in the positive is a very difficult thing to do, especially if there was a time during your childhood when you were truly happy … and then something happened to change it all. Clients often report how frequently things from their generally positive past turned into sad experiences. Basically, they are afraid that if they feel present, positive emotions, something will happen to make those feelings go away. So, instead of savoring the positive feelings in the present, their emotions shift into fearful feelings about the future. Very often people go back and forth from past pain to future fear which keeps them in dysfunction and it negatively affects so many potentially great relationships.

CONSIDER THESE STORIES:

Sally went through an awkward stage as the "new girl" in sixth grade. Her family had just moved to a different state, and it wasn't easy to make friends in January—when friendships and cliques had already been formed. But the day she was invited to a co-ed party at Miranda's house, she was elated. Not only was Miranda the most popular girl in the sixth grade, but she also had a huge group of friends. Sally was confident that this would be her big chance to make some new friends. This was also Sally's first co-ed party and she finally had something to get excited about because all the "popular" kids would be there. Her mother helped Sally select a yellow party dress with black patent leather shoes for the occasion and Sally was absolutely bursting with happiness and anticipation about the event—that is, until she walked into the party. All of the girls were wearing blouses, kilts and penny loafers. Nobody—except for Sally—was wearing patent leather shoes, and her party dress was a glaring departure from the "look" everyone else was wearing. This fashion faux pas made her feel highly embarrassed and those fleeting positive feelings about the party morphed into something negative.

Sally and her mother had also agonized over a gift. She finally decided to give Miranda what she herself would have wanted: an art set, complete with paints, special paper, colored pencils and a "how-to" guide. On the night of the party, Miranda began opening her gifts—and suddenly Sally realized she'd made a terrible mistake: every other girl at the party showered Miranda with gifts of clothing, nail polish and makeup. Before she even opened the gift, Sally had a feeling Miranda wasn't interested in art. From that day on, Sally was fearful and suspicious about any event that promised to be fun and exciting or where groups of people knew each other. She was also very afraid to meet new women, felt insecure and felt that she didn't fit in.

* * *

At the age of six, Billy was a happy-go-lucky boy who loved spending time with his grandfather (who lived with him and his parents). In fact, when his teacher asked the class to make Valentine's cards for special relatives, Billy created a special glitter-covered masterpiece for his grandfather. He practically sprinted home from school that day, ready to give him the card. However, when he walked in the house, his mother rushed over to Billy, giving him a huge hug. Tears streamed down her face as she said, "Billy, Grandpa had a heart attack today, and the doctors couldn't help him. He died." Billy was devastated: How could something so terrible happen? He had just talked to his grandfather that morning and he had seemed completely fine.

From that day forward, he was reluctant to express positive feelings toward loved ones for fear that something awful might happen. In his mind, he prepared to do something nice for his grandfather, and as soon as he did that, something bad happened. Billy wasn't going to take that chance ever again.

* * *

Brian was the star football player at his high school, and everything was going along smoothly: good grades, a caring girlfriend and a strong network *of friends from his football team. Unfortunately, one of Billy's teammates got involved with drugs and alcohol and was tragically killed in a car accident while under the influence. Billy was so distraught over the accident and his friend's death that he stopped playing football.*

* * *

Difficult experiences such as these are universal to us all, along with some uncomfortable emotions—embarrassment, disappointment and heartache. Sometimes, the impact from these experiences leaves lasting scars in the form of distrust and suspicion surrounding the future.

Maybe you have experienced something similar: you were at the peak of your career, or you were blissfully involved with a romantic partner, or you were feeling supreme confidence until something happened to shatter your happiness, relationships and/or self-esteem. If you stay stuck in that pain without learning how to move through and beyond it, you risk losing your awareness and appreciation of the present. Instead, you could vacillate between reliving the negative experiences from your past and fearing the potential catastrophes that you believe are awaiting you in the future.

This negativity can affect all aspects of your life, including important relationships. Let's say that you've met someone who is a perfect match for you. Instead of appreciating the fact that the two of you found each other, you may superimpose all of the negative feelings about your failed relationships from the past on your current partner. You might even sabotage the beginning of a promising relationship for fear that things might not work out in the future.

Your perfect mate may also come from a similar internal experience where fear has trapped him/her and then both of you wind up going into the past pain/future fear cycle. Often couples will take turns—one in the past the other in the future. This makes it doubly difficult and relationships quickly become stagnant.

Is there any escape from this vicious cycle?

Yes, by building and staying in the present. We can become so obsessed with planning and schedules, where we're going next and what our future may hold, that it's difficult to stay centered on the here and now. Add to that the fact that painful past memories may play into your fears about the future, and you've got the makings of a life in which you're only going through the motions but not really being truly "present".

So, how do you stay present? A vital way to do that is through acknowledgement of everyone you appreciate in your life. Become aware of who loves you and begin to trust in that person's love for you. Consider how each person you call to mind touches your soul, your heart and your life. So often we take the people we love for granted, and we end up forgetting how important they are to us. The more often that we express gratitude for our loved ones and the more often we can recall how they touch us, the easier it becomes to regain our trust in the positive.

When we live in the present the past pain and future fear go away!

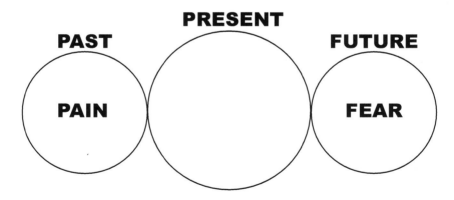

EXERCISE: PRESENT LIVING, SIMPLIFIED

For this exercise, you will need to draw a huge circle in the middle of a piece of paper. Before you go any further take a look at the example here: The small circles of past pain and future fear illustrate the places people go, and the places they get stuck as they go back and forth and back and forth, etc.

1. In the big circle, write down all of the people and things that are important to you in your life at this time. Include friends, relatives, your career, hobbies you enjoy, your faith community, etc.
2. Under each item listed, describe how he/she/it touches your heart and soul. Probe as deeply as you can: tap into your feelings and jot down how important these people and items are to you in the present.
3. Read this list out loud to yourself each night before you go to sleep so that you keep them in your "present." Be sure to draw an X through past pain and future fear and know that you are living in the present.

The more you see and fill up your present with these positive thoughts and feelings, the more you will feel trust. The more you trust that it's OK for you to have these positive feelings, the less likely you are to revert to your past pain or obsess about future fears. Living in the present is the key, because it allows you to appreciate everything and everyone in your life that is important to you. Over time, trusting in the present will begin the process of healing the past pain and eliminating future fear. When that happens, not only will your present moments improve, but you will also look toward your future with positive anticipation and expectancy.

Chapter 10
The Should List

"To thine own self be true."

*- **William Shakespeare***

One day, six-year-old Tom and his little sister were playing "house." As he held the baby doll in his arms, his father stormed into the room. "Tom! What do think you're doing? Boys should play sports—not sit in the house and play with their sister's dolls!"

Tom wondered, What's wrong with me? I thought this was fun, but I guess I shouldn't like playing house with my sister. I guess I shouldn't like playing with dolls, either …

Like Tom in the scenario above, everyone is raised with parents who give them messages that are couched in "should" statements—telling us what we "should" do, how we "should" behave, how we "should" feel and what we "should" do about these feelings. As children, we may blindly follow our parents' advice, even if we don't agree.

"Should" is a value judgment someone has for another person and unfortunately, we sometimes accept these statements as truth right into adulthood. Over time we begin to feel guilty and conflicted when our choices don't mesh with those "shoulds" from childhood. While there may be childhood "shoulds" that are completely in sync with your current beliefs (and therefore are messages that you will want to keep) it is imperative to separate from other people's "should" lists that are *not* aligned to your personal values and lifestyle.

As you consider the "should" messages from your earliest years, you will probably notice that these messages will fall into one of two categories: overt and covert. Overt messages are obvious statements, and they usually include the actual word "should." Here some common examples:

- Children should be seen and not heard.
- You should be polite to adults.
- You should appreciate what you have.
- You shouldn't lie.
- You should not feel, just fix.
- You should not talk back.
- You should not ask why.
- You should clean in a specific way.
- Men should never show their feelings.
- Women should never ask for what they want.

Covert messages, on the other hand, aren't quite so obvious. The "should" isn't present in the statements, though it is implied. You just need to look for it. For instance, I hated my nose as a kid and came home one day crying because I thought it was too big. What I really wanted my mother to say was, "Sweetheart, I think you're beautiful! But all of that doesn't matter; it's who you are on the inside that counts."

Instead of hearing those reassuring words, my mother dismissed my feelings and said, "Well, when you get older, you can get a nose job." This is a covert "should." She was essentially telling me I shouldn't feel but instead should simply intellectualize my feelings away. Over time, this became difficult for me because I began to internalize the message that it was wrong to have feelings. By the time I was in my twenties, I truly didn't know how I felt in any given situation!

As you come across covert statements, do your best to translate the message into a "should" statement so you can shine light on them and begin to eliminate them from your life. Here are some situations and examples of covert messages:

- In response to her hurt feelings, Elise's mother says, "Don't worry about that. You'll get over it soon enough." The hidden "should": *You should not acknowledge uncomfortable feelings; just ignore them and wait for them to go away.*
- Sharon tells her aunt she's planning a new hairstyle. Her aunt says, "Oh, you don't want your hair to look like that!" The hidden "should": *You should trust the opinions of others instead of having your own ideas, because you don't really know what you want.*
- Tom starts crying after his team loses the baseball game. Tom's father tells him to brush it off and says, "Don't be a sissy!" The hidden "should": *Boys shouldn't cry. They should pretend nothing's wrong, even when something is bothering them, or else they are weak "sissies."*
- Raul brings home straight A's in college, and his parents treat him to dinner at his favorite restaurant. At dinner, his parents gush about how proud they are of Raul and that they are making the family proud. The hidden "should": *You should excel in academics, and you should be satisfied with nothing less than the best for yourself.*

THE "SHOULDS" IN YOUR LIFE TODAY

The minute I hear someone say, "You should do thus and such," I know this is about him or her. I know that person is judging me based on his or her own values, thoughts or opinions—projecting what is important to that individual and not what is best for me. No one has the right to "should" another, but people try ... especially adults!

For example, a few months after the birth of my son, the principal of the school at which I taught asked me if I was going to have another baby. I said I hadn't thought about it yet. She said that I should and then launched into a diatribe about why I should have a second child. I realized later that she only had one child and was disappointed because she'd always wanted more children. She "should-ed" me based on *her* life, not mine.

The next time you interact with a "should-er," listen closely. While he or she is busy "should-ing" you, you will find that the other person's truth is what eventually comes out. You can even ask him or her questions about why you "should" do whatever is being suggested to you as you begin to ferret out that person's hidden agenda. Even well-meaning advice in the form of "shoulds" is still about the other person's reality and not about you. It doesn't mean the person doesn't care about you. In fact, sometimes the people who care about you deeply will "should" you the most! However, it is not your responsibility to integrate their "shoulds" into your life ... unless *you* agree with them.

Parents constantly tell their children what they should be doing, such as, "You should keep your room clean at all times" or, "You should do the dishes after eating!" That's funny, because most children don't think they "should" be doing these activities, but their parents do! The kiddos have different priorities; so again, it's all about the parents' "should."

Yes, parents are obligated to teach their children responsibility, how to function in society and how to contribute to their community, but it needs to be in an "I" statement format.

Husbands and wives also frequently "should" each other: "She should have dinner ready every night since she's not working" or, "He should help more with the cleaning and the kids." And on and on it goes!

To be clear, if what you're asking another person to do relates to something that you need to have accomplished, then make an "I" statement instead, in order to keep your message clear.

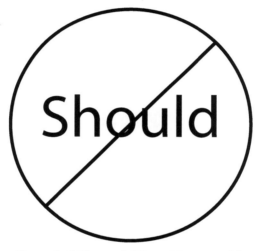

Don't "Should" on Yourself

EXERCISE: YOU "SHOULD" DO THIS.

1. List the "shoulds" from your past. Think back to all the "shoulds" your mom and dad gave you. You'll probably notice that there are some statements that you disagree with and dislike, while there may be other statements you deem noble, right, virtuous, etc. At this point, don't judge any of the statements—just list them.

2. Separate the messages. Review what you've written. Place a check mark next to the statements that you honestly agree with. What this will do is force you to separate yourself from your family of origin. In other words, you will finally establish the "shoulds" that work for you—and not just because you had a "should" imposed on you. This exercise also frees you up to release the messages you don't agree with and those that don't serve you well.

    Note: It is possible that as you begin to identify messages that are not part of your values (a.k.a., not on your personal "should" list) you may feel guilty—as if you're betraying family members for not clinging to the messages they imposed on you. Understand, that this isn't a matter of loyalty to *people*: if you choose to hang onto messages that you don't need or agree with, you're basically being loyal to *dysfunction*.

3. Throw it out! The more you work with your list, the more you'll come to realize that familial "shoulds" were learned. Just as you can learn any skill or concept, you can also unlearn it. Think about any subject that you

learned in school where you knew the information for the test, yet promptly forgot about that information as soon as you turned it in. Most likely the information wasn't something all that important to you or your life. It wasn't going to make a difference to you and therefore you never really owned it. It's the same with your family-imposed "should" messages: any message given to you by your parents or other family members, no matter how well meaning, really has nothing to do with you. These are "shoulds" that your mother, father, and other significant family members valued, and wanted you to value as well.

As an adult *you* get to choose. Remember if you find "should" statements on the list that you agree with and that are congruent with your lifestyle and value system, then by all means keep those statements. A useful way to do this is to ask yourself whose voice is it when you say something with "should" in it. Is it an internal parent's voice or your own? Now you can take conscious ownership of those "shoulds". However, if it's a message you don't agree with or one that contradicts the way you want to live your life, then you might want *get rid of it*. To do this, ask yourself how this "should" serves you in your life. Does it limit you? What would you gain if you let it go? What stops you from doing that? Any fears?

4. Remember the "I" statement. Consider what you truly want and need in your life, and then express yourself to others in that way. This will come in handy for you

when you work to integrate the "shoulds" in your life that you want to keep.

If you feel it's important to respect your elders, then make that clear when you're tempted to "should" someone. Instead of saying, "You should respect me because I'm fifty years older than you!" you could reframe it as: "I feel confident that I have life experience and wisdom in this situation, and I would like my point of view to be considered." This is more than semantics; it's sharing your deepest feelings and values with the other person without trying to impose your belief system on him or her.

5. If you are part of a couple each of you is to make your "should" list and share it with each other. Identify how each other's "shoulds" have affected the other. Share which "should" you each want to eliminate and kindly help each other in the process of making the changes.

FINAL THOUGHTS: THE HYPOCRITICAL "SHOULDS"

Be cognizant of the paradoxical "shoulds" on your list. Once, I had a couple create their own lists individually, and then they shared their lists in a therapy session. One of the items on the husband's list was, "Men should not objectify women." He then told me that it was time for him to talk to his son about porn—about how bad it is, not to look at it, etc. His wife immediately rolled her eyes at him and laughed. When I asked her to explain why she was laughing, she said, "I just think it's pretty funny that he's going to tell Adam not to look at porn when he looks at porn himself."

His wife had a point: how can he teach his son not to do something when he's doing it himself? While the wife was not judging him about his habit her point was that his "should" statement is incongruous with his personal lifestyle. While that particular message would come from a well-meaning family member, he needs to come up with a better way to frame it so that it is not at odds with his personal actions. Otherwise he is creating unnecessary conflict within himself—and sending his son a mixed message in the process.

If the message he wants to convey to his son is about respecting women then he wants to consider what he actually *does* and share *that* information with his son. Maybe he is a good listener when his wife is sharing her day with him; in that case, he could teach his son active listening skills. Or maybe he always does thoughtful little things to show his wife that he's thinking of her (a kind text, a surprise night out to dinner, volunteering to carpool when it was her turn, etc.). He may want to explain to his son how those small, respectful gestures mean a lot to a loved one. Note that in these examples, everything he would share with his son parallels his own actions and therefore creates a powerful message that would be difficult for their son to ignore.

"Actions speak louder than words" is more than a cliché. To come to terms with the "shoulds" that *truly* resonate with you—while dismissing the messages that don't—will allow you to live more authentically and in a way that is aligned with your personal value system. Your relationships will also get better as you become clearer on who you are and how you want to lead your life.

Chapter 11
Prepare, Don't Repair

"An ounce of prevention is worth a pound of cure."

- Ben Franklin

Every day when Josh started his car, it made a strange grinding sound. However, Josh was one to typically run late in the morning and never had enough time to investigate. Then, by the end of the day, he would forget all about his car and the weird noise.

One morning about two weeks later, Josh turned the key in the ignition. Nothing. After ten frantic minutes of trying to get the car to start, Josh called the mechanic who told him the grinding noise he mentioned definitely had something to do with the car not starting. "I'll need to tow it to the garage, and then we can give you a loaner. Should only take about an hour to get a truck out to your house."

Josh cringed. He didn't have an hour. He was scheduled to meet with an important client and his part of the presentation was set to begin at 9:00 a.m. sharp. He groaned as the mechanic said what he already knew: "If you had brought your car in two weeks ago, you wouldn't be having this problem today!"

Just like car maintenance, preventive techniques are critical in maintaining a positive relationship with your partner. I'd much rather you treat each other with love, kindness and respect in the first place than hurt one another and then later apologize. Unfortunately it's all too common to see people apologize—and then continue to do the same hurtful behaviors again.

The goal of this chapter is to share concepts that will create an environment in which you don't need to *repair* your relationship; instead, you can spend time *preparing* to make the relationship successful. Many people come to see me because they need techniques designed to repair their relationship. Ideally it's always easier if you can pave the way for success so that you don't get to that point. Even with something as simple as a car repair, it's easy to see that when you address issues as you spot them you take proactive steps which prevent pain further down the road.

One of the most common issues couples have is that each partner is often apologizing for their thoughtless words or actions ... but then they continue the same hurtful behaviors, over and over. The key to preventing this situation to begin with is to be conscious in one's communications and actions.

Once I had a client who told me he had OTM. "What is that?" I had asked.

He responded, "On the mind, out the mouth." This gentleman is not alone. Too many people have bad cases of "OTM"—and that's what is causing the majority of their problems with significant others.

The first thing you can do to stop hurting one another is to *think first* before speaking. Sounds easy, doesn't it? While this deceptively simple piece of advice is unbelievably powerful. I can't tell you how many people intuitively know that they should think before speaking—but they don't follow through with it.

Yes, it's important to be open and honest with your partner, but sharing what's on your mind the second a thought pops into your head doesn't always work. The timing and sensitivity just isn't there. However, if you process what you're thinking and feeling and take some time to consider your words before broaching the subject with your partner, your interactions with your partner can be truly transformative.

FRAMES OF REFERENCE

Being more deliberate before speaking doesn't mean that you don't share your feelings. Rather, you become more purposeful and deliberate about *when* and *how* you share information. Conscious thought is all part of learning the other person's frame of reference. In other words, you need to be aware of what hurts the other person. This skill is critical, because learning each other's frame of reference is one of the major keys to opening the door to a successful, loving relationship. Frame of reference includes how the other person thinks, processes, expresses himself/herself and shares. It also includes how easy or difficult it is for him or her to share deep feelings, be vulnerable, etc.

For instance, let's say that your spouse wants you to remind her not to snack because she's trying to lose some weight. A few days after you agree to help her be "accountable," you see her at the cookie jar. Your first instinct is to say something like, "There you go again, breaking your New Year's resolution!" or "Remember, a minute on the lips means a lifetime on the hips!" Not surprisingly, uttering any of these words to your wife will most likely be met with anger or reproach.

But, you might be thinking, *she asked me to remind her not to snack So,* be conscious of what you're going to say—and how you're going to say it. Consider your wife's personality. If you know she's super-sensitive, don't remind her with a sarcastic comment or flippant jab. That's not going to motivate her; it's just going to hurt her feelings. Instead, you might say something like, "Honey, do you still want me to remind you about the snacking?" Notice that you've helped her by indicating to her that you've noticed she's snacking, but you haven't made a value judgment or made her feel bad in the process.

At this point, your wife might have had a change of heart: she really *doesn't* want the reminders. Or, maybe she does and your polite question is all she needs. Notice that in this scenario, you're still communicating openly with your spouse, but you've done so in a way that is much more likely to garner positive feelings and appreciation.

My client Sarah shared a great example of how she learned her husband's frame of reference when she asked him if he had watered the lawn. He said yes, but three days later she noticed the side yard was turning brown. She said to him, "I thought you watered the lawn!"

"I did," he responded.

"Then why is the side yard brown?"

"I watered the front yard!"

In this case, Sarah realized that her husband was a literal thinker, while she was much more global. In her mind, watering the lawn meant watering all zones. For him, watering the lawn meant he watered one zone only.

Understanding her husband's frame of reference has prevented many future conflicts, because now Sarah knows that if she asks a question, she needs to be clearer (by asking "Did you water all zones of the lawn?") rather than assuming he knows what she means. And her husband realizes that that when Sarah asks a question about watering the lawn she means "every zone."

My client, Mike, learned that his frame of reference and his wife's were dramatically different when it came to how they prepared for Christmas gift giving. Mike was brought up with a tradition where most of the gifts are hidden until Christmas Eve; this would build suspense and make the sudden appearance of all the gifts under the tree more dramatic. Plus, Mike enjoyed trying to find those hidden gifts prior to Christmas Eve, too. Meanwhile, his wife was brought up with the gifts being wrapped and placed under the tree weeks in advance; this would get Sally excited about the anticipation of opening all of those wonderful presents!

Imagine the disappointment both felt when Mike saw all his gifts proudly displayed under the tree—rather than carefully hidden away until the big moment. Sally couldn't believe that Mike only bought her one or two gifts—which wasn't true, as Sally didn't know that Mike had the other gifts hidden in the basement. Until the two of them discussed their feelings and traditions, neither one realized that they were unwittingly upsetting the other person. In fact, they thought they were creating anticipation for the other person! They were both doing Christmas the way they each wanted it done.

Understanding each other's frame of reference has allowed the couple to be more sensitive to the other's preferences in the future, even for something as simple as gift-wrapped presents at Christmas time. Now, Sally keeps her gifts hidden, while Mike is sure to display all of Sally's gifts well before December 25th. Both of them enjoy keeping their childhood traditions alive, and this compromise doesn't diminish either one's personal preferences. Now Sally enjoys seeing how excited Mike is about waiting for his gifts to appear on Christmas Eve and Mike loves seeing Sally's excitement as she tries to guess what's in those boxes.

Another example of learning the other person's frame of reference comes from Jeff. He had a horrible habit of interrupting his wife and coworkers while they were talking. Jeff was one of seven children and as a child he wasn't given the chance to be heard as much as he needed to be. As a result, his habit of interrupting was very important to him because he needed to be heard and didn't know any other way to get attention. Fortunately, once he became aware of his habit, he started practicing being still while his wife spoke until it was his turn to talk. At first, it was difficult for him to trust that he would get his "chance," but with time he realized that not only could he be heard but he could also respect what other people had to say by being a polite listener.

Notice that in all of these examples each partner becomes more attuned to his or her own emotional "hot buttons" (being overly sensitive, being a literal thinker, valuing childhood traditions, etc.), and the end result is two-pronged: each partner becomes more sensitive to the needs and desires of the other person, and each individual learns his or her own preferences and needs as well. Just being aware of what you want and need will make it much clearer when it comes to understanding why you have such strong emotional reactions to certain personalities and situations.

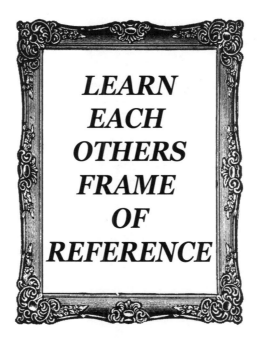

LEARN EACH OTHERS FRAME OF REFERENCE

EXERCISE: SHARING LEADS TO CARING

Below are some simple steps you can take to prepare—not repair—your relationships:

1. Make a list of your emotional triggers. These could include such things as the tone or volume of the other person's voice; lack of eye contact when talking; constantly answering the phone while spending time together; text messaging while listening to the other person; or anything else that you find hurtful.

2. Share. Exchange your list with your partner. Note where your perceptions do and don't match. Remember, there are no right or wrong answers—just the realization that perceptions are what matter, and this communication will open up a world of possibilities for improving your relationship.

3. Prepare. In future interactions, keep your partner's list in mind as you communicate. For example, if you know that speaking loudly and forcefully upsets your spouse, commit to speaking in softer tones as much as possible. Or, if your partner has a need to be taken seriously in certain situations, refrain from making sarcastic comments that may undermine him/her when discussing those issues/topics.

REWIND, REWORD.

This technique is an excellent one to use if you notice that you're being triggered in a situation. Instead of storming out of the room, breaking down in tears or reacting with anger, simply ask the other person to "rewind" and/or "reword" what he or she just said.

For example, if you are becoming defensive because your partner's body language or tone triggers you, you could say, "Please rewind." This signals to your partner that you are perceiving the other person to be angry or aggressive in some way and you are feeling uncomfortable.

Some people don't feel the necessity to rewind because they insist their intentions are good, but the partner's *perception* is the key. To that person you may be coming off as explosive or threatening. Being able to rewind is a way to "take two" and express yourself with a style that the other person is able to receive well.

Asking your partner to "reword" is another signal you can use if you are reacting to *what* the person said. To revisit the example about the wife who was dieting and wanted reminders if she snacked, she could have said, "I need that reworded." This would alert her husband that his sarcastic comment wasn't helping, but if he reworded his message in a different way then she might respond more favorably.

Rewind, reword helps the other person realize that you're interpreting what they're trying to say in a hurtful or judgmental way. With this technique, the person who is being asked to reword or rewind has to acknowledge that the person is interpreting the words in a certain way—whether intentionally or not. Even if your intention is not to be hurtful or judgmental, you can't defend yourself during this exercise. You just need to know that the other person is interpreting it and it is triggering them so you honor it and reword or rewind.

Many couples find themselves in situations where there are other people around when comments are made and they don't feel comfortable saying "reword" or "rewind" out loud. In this case, you can use a signal.

I usually have clients hold up two fingers, which indicates to the other person that he or she has interpreted something to be judgmental or was stated in an angry way. The two fingers means he or she needs the message reworded or rewound. I know this can be frustrating for the person who doesn't believe they did or said anything "wrong" but the fact remains that the other person has expressed that what was said did result in negative feelings. In fact, the partner should be encouraged to share details *later*. The important point is that *at the time it is happening,* it is best just to reword or rewind.

ALL IN THE FAMILY

Rewind, reword can also be used by all family members. If children perceive that their mother is yelling at them they can hold up two fingers. Whether she is yelling, raising her voice or speaking firmly is not as important as the children's perception of the communication. They indicate their discomfort with their hand signal—an unspoken request to immediately stop and reword what she's trying to say without yelling (or change her tone of voice and/or body language). She can then restate what she needs to so that the children can listen to her. If you implement this technique with your family, however, be sure that your children understand they may not use the technique as manipulation. They really need to be honest and only use it if they truly feel that they are being yelled at inappropriately.

GOOD INTENTIONS

It is important to understand that, most of the time, people are unaware of their body language and tone of voice when they're communicating. In addition, there are typically unfinished issues from the past that cause some frustration.

I believe that most people who care for one another don't *intend* to hurt one another. Intention is very important and trusting that the people you care for have your best interests at heart is an important idea to remember. Most have heard the expression "the road to hell is paved with good intentions," but I also believe the road to heaven is filled with good intentions. We simply need to act from our good intentions.

EXERCISE: PLEASE BE KIND, REWIND

Here's a recap of how to use *rewind, reword* in your communications and interactions:

1. Remember your triggers. Keep your emotional trigger list (from the exercise earlier in this chapter) handy. The next time you find yourself in a situation where you partner's words or body language creates emotional distress for you, ask him or her to "rewind" or "reword."

2. Ask for a "rewind" if triggered by nonverbal communication which includes tone of voice, body language, etc. If your partner is coming across as angry, aggressive or hostile, ask him/her to "rewind." That signals your partner that he or she must approach you with a different tone of voice, posture, etc.

3. Ask for a "reword" if the message is upsetting you. This includes the words the person has chosen to use. So, if you are upset by those words, express that to your partner. If you say, "Please reword that," then your partner knows that he or she can still express himself/ herself, but it just needs to be worded in a different way. Many couples find it helpful to use a signal for rewind or reword instead of saying those words. Some examples include holding up a baby finger or tugging on one's earlobe.

Practice, practice, practice. Sometimes it's easy to brush off your feelings, especially if it's not *that* hurtful or *that* painful. However, remember that if you don't prepare by taking proactive steps to communicate positively with your partner, chances are good that eventually you're going to need to repair the relationship.

The best part is that the more seasoned you and your partner become at asking the other person to rewind or reword, the less frequently you will find yourself using this strategy. With practice, your partner will become much more sensitive to your needs and therefore will automatically begin changing his/her words, body language and tone of voice. Eventually, internalizing these skills will make interactions with your partner not only more effective, but you will also find yourself enjoying the time that you spend together more than you could imagine.

Chapter 12
Accept, Don't Expect

"Happiness can exist only in acceptance."

- George Orwell

Ted has been married to Barbara for ten years, and early on in their marriage she noticed something about her husband: Ted needs a long time to get ready to go out. It doesn't matter if he's running to the gym or preparing for a job interview; he always seems to need that hour—or else he gets completely frazzled.

For their anniversary, Barbara has decided to surprise Ted with a trip to an island. As he walks through the door after work, she squeals, "Surprise!" and presents him with two plane tickets to the Virgin Islands. Ted gives Barbara a huge hug and turns toward the staircase.

"Where are you going?" Barbara asks.

"I'm going to get ready to go," Ted explains.

"But we don't have time, Ted! Our flight's in two hours. We need to leave for the airport now!" Noting Ted's look of consternation, Barbara finds herself getting annoyed.

What's up with him? *Barbara thinks.* I bend over backwards planning this trip, and his thank you is that he needs his precious hour to get ready? Can't he just let go of it for once and simply walk out to the car?!

Meanwhile, Ted can't understand why Barbara is so upset. She knows I need extra time to prepare for something as special as a trip! *He thinks.* And even though she packed my bags, I still need some time to shave, take a shower ...

The issue of Ted's need for extra time and Barbara's annoyance at this need is a classic example of what can happen when one partner can't accept certain aspects in the other partner's personality. Barbara has been with Ted for a decade, yet she still hasn't completely accepted his need to have extra time to prepare to leave the house. Her refusal to accept Ted's need is going to create tension on an occasion that should be a happy one.

While Barbara does not need to love this aspect of Ted's personality, continuing to fight her husband in this area is setting both of them up for disappointment.

My solution? Accept, don't expect.

You may be thinking, "that sounds way too simple to make a difference," but this statement has served my clients well over the years. When we accept the limitations of the people we come in contact with, they don't disappoint us. When we accept their limitations, we are not expecting them to betray who they truly are. By accepting *what is* and not expecting *what could be*, we become less vulnerable.

In the case of Barbara and Ted, it's clearly thoughtful and generous for Barbara to plan the trip, yet she already knows Ted needs time to prepare for anything and everything. So in this instance, both partners would be best served by allotting some measure of extra time—even if it's a token amount—so that the two can enjoy the surprise without conflict and tension. Maybe they could take a later flight or perhaps they could have arranged for Ted to come home early that day. The point is that by simply accepting Ted's need for time, and then planning accordingly, lots of unnecessary stress could be avoided. Many times, going that extra step doesn't take much additional time or effort, but the payback is immense. Both partners can be free to be who they are and there's no unnecessary strain on the relationship to navigate.

As you read this, you may be thinking, *Barbara's already made this huge effort to plan a trip! Can't Ted adjust?* Ted's actions aren't meant to diminish Barbara's gesture. And while it's possible for Ted to "let it go" for once, chances are good that he won't and Barbara probably already knows this. In their relationship, this has always been a sticking point for them. Ignoring the issue only causes the same conflict over and over.

There are probably aspects of your partner's personality or habits that are not going to change much. It doesn't really matter how silly you might think these foibles are, but a refusal to accept these aspects are what leads to tension and strife. Rather than thinking of it as giving in or giving up, you can *choose* to accept certain situations and make *your* life easier and more enjoyable in the process! Acceptance doesn't make you a doormat, it empowers you to choose your battles and allow life to become more pleasant.

Our everyday lives are filled with opportunities to take control and avoid unnecessary aggravation, even in the most mundane situations. For example:

- If you accept the fact that when you go through a fast food drive-through it may be difficult to hear or that you will be interrupted when giving your order, then you are much less likely to get frustrated and short-tempered when this actually happens. Instead, you will simply enjoy the overall convenience that such a facility provides and leave with a smile.

- If you, as an employee, know that your boss is task-oriented, then you know not to expect a touchy-feely humanistic approach when discussing new challenges on the job.
- If you, as a spouse, know that you married a single-tasker, don't expect to suddenly find a multi-tasker as your mate. Plan ahead to avoid feeling hurt or disappointed. If you want to discuss something important, select a time when both of you will be refreshed and ready to listen. Don't set yourself up for failure.
- If you, as a parent, know that your child has an average IQ, then don't expect to see above-average grades, thereby setting the stage for personal insecurities, self-doubt, low self-esteem, etc. This doesn't mean you let your child squeak by, but rather ask him/her to put forth effort and see where that leads. With your guidance and support, each child can develop the traits and characteristics that make him or her unique, blossoming into a fully functional adult in the process.

There are times when we do not recognize that our partners are willing and attempting to make a change. I've heard women complain, "Oh, my husband will never listen to me!" and husbands have voiced similar complaints, such as, "She'll never change her mind on that one …" However, when couples make a sincere effort to work on the relationship, the potential is limitless.

At the same time, you must be realistic and understand that someone's innate temperament and personality is not likely to undergo a complete and total transformation. If you're married to an introvert, you probably can't expect him or her to ever want to become the life of the party. And if you are looking to "tone down" your gregarious partner, understand that there may be a limit to your expectations. You fell in love with that person for who he or she is. If you accept your partner for his or her strengths and weaknesses, it will be much easier for your partner to accept your positives and negatives, too.

For those of you who are considering marriage, know the limitations of your future mate beforehand, and make sure you can live with those limitations. Do not get married with the hidden agenda that you can change him or her. Be sure the issues that bother you are tolerable and remember, *accept, don't expect*. Life then becomes an adventure to be enjoyed together.

When considering what to accept, it is important to note that acceptance doesn't mean that you tolerate abuse or allow people to walk all over you. While you should always take appropriate action to preserve your dignity and self-worth, you can't expect your partner to become something that he or she is not. And if you are involved in a difficult relationship and you don't know if things can ever change, you may need to reevaluate whether you want to work on the relationship or not. Naturally, if your relationship is an abusive one, then it's critical that you take *immediate* action to protect yourself and any children. Accepting abuse is never an option.

The bottom line is to assess each situation separately. Accept the reality of what is; acknowledge the perceptions that are real for the other person and work within those limitations. They cannot change just because you want them to, any more than you can for them. Once you accept this concept, you will not expect a fairytale ending but rather, will be able to relax and enjoy living in the loving reality you are building together.

You are Cordially Invited

to

ACCEPT

what is...

Don't

Expect

any changes

EXERCISE: WHAT TO EXPECT WHEN YOU'RE ACCEPTING

1. List the issues. Think about personality traits and situations that are unlikely to change in your partner. For example, if your spouse is an avid sports fan, you know that he or she loves to go to sporting events and/or watch professional sports on television frequently.

2. Determine which traits/situations you can begin to accept. If your partner's personality trait isn't harmful to you or to others, consider accepting that aspect of his/her personality rather than trying to fight it or change it. For the sports lover, that may mean that you accept that he likes to golf every Saturday. Instead of turning each Saturday morning into an argument, think about things you can do with all that extra time by yourself or with other friends. Rather than resenting your time apart, you can cultivate individual interests and suggest he routinely commit to spending Sunday with you! Or, maybe you'll decide to learn the sport yourself so that you can occasionally join him on the green!

Maybe your wife loves long phone calls with friends. Instead of nagging her to get off the phone, use that time to take a nap, watch some television or spend time with the kids. Respecting her preferences frees you up to spend your energy on other pursuits. If there is a situation at some point in time where you need to ask her to cut the conversation short, she's more likely to do so, knowing it is the exception and not the rule.

Allowing that change is the only constant in life, accept what is and enjoy what comes. You will be amazed at the outcome of consistently discussing things honestly and respectfully. Trust builds exponentially as each individual feels heard, thus providing the basis for a lasting relationship.

Chapter 13
To Argue or Not to Argue

"Discussion is an exchange of knowledge; an argument an exchange of ignorance."

- Robert Quillen

To argue or not to argue, that is the question. I can't tell you how many times people have come to me and said that they heard that fighting/arguing is good for a relationship. I'm here to tell you otherwise: fighting causes tempers to flare and eventually leads to people saying hurtful things they don't mean. Bickering, nagging, nitpicking—all of it—ends up in circular conversations. That's because arguing provides no positive outcome.

I have been told by clients that they thought they were supposed to fight with the one they love. "Aren't they the ones we can do this with" NO! Remember the first line of the song from the Mills Brothers, "You Always Hurt the One You Love?" The first line is the same as the title and the second line is "… the one you shouldn't hurt at all." People remember that first line and not the second. There is truly nothing healthy about fighting. Arguing, fighting, reacting and exploding are the things that are most dangerous to relationships.

Consider the case of Paul and Amanda:

Paul loves "toys" from boats to electronics to sports equipment. If it's the latest and greatest, Paul wants it. Amanda, on the other hand, is more conservative with her money. She was raised in a family that valued financial security; saving for retirement, emergencies and "rainy days" were common topics of discussion growing up. So whenever Paul comes home with a new gadget, Amanda flies off the handle. Not only can't she believe that Paul has spent an exorbitant amount of money on an item that she fails to see the value of, but he also never even discusses it with her prior to making the purchase! Amanda wonders how they can ever save for their futures if he spends their paychecks as quickly as they earn them.

Paul and Amanda's constant arguments get them nowhere. Instead of coming to terms with the issue, Amanda yells at Paul and then sulks. Meanwhile, Paul fights back initially, but then he simply endures the nagging, knowing it will eventually blow over. After a day or two, Amanda caves in and starts talking to Paul again and then things return to normal—until Paul brings home another purchase.

I'm not saying Amanda and Paul should not *disagree*. On the contrary, each person has the right to his or her opinion about anything and everything. However, my goal is to have couples explain their thoughts, opinions and feelings in a way that allows each person to be heard without the hidden agenda of being "right." There is no right or wrong in such discussions. There are simply different perspectives—different ways of viewing things.

In the above instance, Paul is certainly entitled to enjoy his "toys," while Amanda has every right to enjoy the security she finds in saving money. The dysfunction lies in the way the two assert their positions: Amanda thinks the only way to "win" is to transform Paul's saving habits.

Meanwhile, Paul resists Amanda's attempts at "conversion" for fear that he will never again be able to enjoy fun splurges.

To Argue or Not to Argue

COMPROMISE: A BETTER OPTION

Compromise is not always easy, but it is more productive and effective than fighting. Compromise allows you to grow as a couple. You can try to convince the other person why your viewpoint is important and why you want him or her to agree with you, but in the end you may need to compromise if you can't both agree.

You have the right to share your thoughts, feelings and opinions, but it is equally important that you *listen* to each other. Recognize that what the other person is saying is real for him or her. Understand that you don't have to agree with them ,unless you truly see things the same way! Instead, simply acknowledge that what the other is saying is important to him or her. At that point, you can enter a new arena of compromise. It's critical to validate your partner's feelings. Listening also ensures that your partner will trust you.

Compromise may mean that Paul agrees to consult Amanda before making his next purchase. Perhaps Amanda won't be as resistant if she felt she were included in the decision-making process. Maybe Paul is willing to wait until the item goes on sale and put the difference between the sales price and original price into their savings account. Or maybe the couple agrees to a set aside a certain percentage of their paychecks for savings each month; any remainder can then be used for splurges. The actual solution isn't as important as the fact that both partners are empathizing with one another and they are willing to remain flexible in a way that benefits them both.

Compromise is truly an art. Considering both "sides" and blending them together in a way that works for both people doesn't always come naturally, but the benefits are well worth it!

WHEN COMPROMISE DOESN'T WORK

When compromise proves impossible, you may need to enter that topic into a new category. My husband and I found an additional category works well in these situations. We call it the "Drop It" category. We use it when one of us wants to do or have something that the partner believes is too pricey, too dangerous or is diametrically opposed to that person's values. The person who wants something can use as much persuasion and try to convince the other that it's a good decision. The other listens carefully but if he/she still doesn't agree he/she simply says "No."—In this situation, when the partner says "No," it's time to drop it (at least, for the time being).

Here is an example of this. My husband wanted to landscape the yard at our new house right away after moving in. I was opposed and was focused on installing blinds instead. He talked, shared, explained and ultimately convinced me because he had good reasons. Although I didn't want the landscaping, he really did. However, if I had said "No" he would have dropped the subject.

I remember trying to convince my husband that getting a pool for the backyard was a great idea. I tried *everything*. He said "No" so I had to drop it.

There are some instances where one partner knows that they cannot compromise. An example of this would be if my husband wanted to buy a motorcycle. I feel strongly that I could never get comfortable with the inherent safety issues and so I would emphatically reply, "No." That means no more motorcycle discussion. Here's another example: once I really wanted to buy a company's stock that my husband considered was too pricey. He was so adamantly against it that he gave me the "No." Subject dropped.

EXERCISE: COUPLES COMPROMISE

The next time you find yourself in conflict with your partner, work through these steps instead of starting an argument:

1. Stop and breathe. Take a "time out." Take a few deep breaths. Don't speak. Pausing for a moment before proceeding to Step Two will allow you to regain composure and prevent you from reacting before thinking. Remember, arguments get you nowhere!

2. Listen. Listen to what your partner has to say. Put yourself in his/her shoes. Understand why your partner feels the way he/she does. You don't have to agree, but you need to accept that your partner's feelings are *real.*

3. Share. Now it's your turn. Share your feelings, and ask your partner to listen as you just have. Make it clear that you don't need agreement, but you do need acknowledgement for your feelings (see Chapter Five on validation for other ideas).

4. Compromise. Here's where you try to find a compromise that works for both of you. Think outside of the box and generate as many solutions as possible. Be sure you can both live with the compromise before agreeing on a course of action or else one (or both) of you might be tempted to back out of the agreement. A great question to ask your partner is what it means for them to get what they want. Once you know the answer to this, the frame of possibilities that may be agreeable to both of you becomes much larger.

5. Wait ... or drop it. If you truly can't compromise, consider tabling the issue for discussion in a few hours or days. When you revisit the situation, it's possible you will have generated more ideas, or you might not feel as emotional about the issue anymore and may be in a more agreeable state than before. However, if you really can't find a happy medium, agree to drop it—at least for now.

6. Rinse and repeat. Continue these steps for all situations that previously devolved into arguments. With practice, compromise and actively listening to your partner will become second nature. Over time, you'll appreciate the fact that you can have a healthy, communicative relationship—without arguments.

Chapter 14
No One Can Enter Your Tornado

"How people treat you is their karma; how you react is yours."

- Wayne Dyer

Julia and Bob were both in their home office. Bob was busy working on the computer and Julia was sitting on the couch. She was trying unsuccessfully, to initiate a conversation with Bob, but he was in the middle of working on an important project for a client that was due the next morning.

After the third attempt to draw Bob out on how his day went, Julia stood up and shouted, "I can't believe you're doing this! You always ignore me. No matter how hard I try, you just keep doing the same thing, over and over. You're too busy on your precious computer to care about your wife!" And before Bob could even respond, she stormed out of the room.

Julia has entered what I call "the tornado." Like a raging storm, something has triggered anger in her and anyone in her path is going to be the victim of destruction—in the form of a verbal attack. Just as a devastating tornado can't be stopped—or dealt with—until the event is over, it is impossible for anyone to do anything about Julia's fury until it's over.

To handle these all-too-common situations for couples, I suggest an approach that is an adaptation from Albert Ellis' Rational Emotive Therapy. In my (similar but not identical) approach, I label each event in the drama that unfolds as follows: the activating event, the feeling, and the reaction to the feeling. In the case of Julia and Bob, I would list these letters on my whiteboard and proceed from there.

Stop! Don't Enter that Tornado

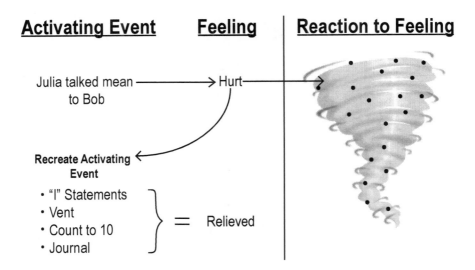

Obviously, the activating event is that Bob ignored Julia. I wrote just that on the board when working with this couple. Then, I asked Julia, "How did that make you feel?"

She responded, "Pissed off!"

This reaction—feeling angry, "pissed off," etc.—is typical, but at this point I'll stop the client because as I mentioned earlier in this book, *anger isn't a feeling*. Anger is a behavior that results from someone being hurt or afraid, or other feelings within those two categories. Anger in and of itself is not an acceptable answer when identifying feelings that follow the activating event.

I probed further: "Julia, anger isn't a feeling. You reacted in anger, but how did you feel when Bob ignored you?"

At that point, tears came to her eyes. "I felt really hurt. He just ignored me. It saddens me to think I am not important enough to talk to."

Now, what happened in this case is that Julia felt hurt, and she moved from the event to the feeling to the reaction to the feeling—which became the "tornado." Interestingly, this chain reaction is nothing new. This exercise allowed the couple to realize that anytime in the past that Julia has felt hurt—no matter what the activating event was—she would enter a huge tornado. And once she's in the tornado, Julia remembers and re-feels all the times Bob ever did something similar in the past—and that's the debris inside that tornado.

As she calls to mind all of the times he's ignored her, those hurt feelings have now morphed into anger, pure anger. Now the anger is in the tornado along with even more debris from the past—other issues and/or the same issues—all at the same time.

The goal of this process is to draw a line between the feeling and the reaction to the feeling. This will allow Julia to identify what she is really feeling and not move it to the tornado. If she enters the tornado it doesn't matter what Bob does or says, Julia will just fly off the handle at him, even if he apologizes, expresses remorse, etc. Worst of all, one person's tornado will oftentimes trigger a tornado in the other person. Now there are two tornadoes, and neither individual is going to get to the root feeling. True feelings are not being acknowledged and everyone's caught up in their own angry whirlwind.

Instead, Julia needs to break the cycle. She must go back to the activating event and create a new activating event. For instance, she could make her "I" statements, or she could vent her feelings in a healthy way by screaming into a pillow, journaling or simply counting to ten and then revisiting the activating event. Most of the time, however, simply focusing on the "I" statement—"I'm feeling really ignored and hurt"—is enough to deal with the activating event in a healthy manner and stop someone from jumping into that dysfunctional tornado.

When I did this exercise with Julia and Bob, Bob mentioned that if had he known how hurt Julia felt, he would have stopped in his tracks. He didn't even realize he was ignoring her. He thought she was just hanging around with him, spending time in the same room. He had no idea her presence was a means of connection until she made her "I" statements. In his mind they do lots of things together—like sitting in the same room where he's playing a game on his laptop and she's on Facebook—and he assumed this was just like those other times. But for some reason, she had taken it in a different way on that particular occasion and now she felt hurt.

Interestingly, when you stop yourself and deal with the activating event using an "I" statement, most partners will listen. You will then feel relieved that you were able to express your true feelings (rather than suppress them or worse, transform true emotions into the behavior of anger). Your own acceptance and comprehension of your feelings by altering the activating event will directly correlate to transforming that feeling of hurt and replace it by relief.

Now if Bob doesn't listen to her "I" statement, then Julia will need to vent. This is when she may need to scream into a pillow or journal her feelings. Even if he doesn't validate her, Julia's own realization of her true feelings will actually tend to make her feel better (with or without the validation from Bob). But know this, most partners *will* validate their partner's feeling, and it is rare for a partner *not* to do so. Usually, the partner will realize, "Oh, my gosh! This is what is bothering her. Now I know." Note that the partner feels relieved, too, because even though the other person is upset and hurt, it is clear to both partners how each individual feels. No one likes being in the dark, and the "I" statements eliminate that confusion.

EXERCISE: STOP THE TORNADO, FIND THE CALM CENTER

This exercise will help you learn to stop yourself before entering a tornado:

1. Hit pause. If your partner does something that causes you to feel hurt, sad, ignored, depressed, etc. you need to recognize that and take a moment to pause. Here are some tell-tale physical signs to clue you in that you're being triggered: feeling sick to your stomach, noticing you're clenching your jaw or fist, feeling your muscles tighten in your neck or face, etc.

2. Identify the feeling. Once you take a moment to pause, check in with yourself. Ask yourself how you're feeling—and don't accept "I feel angry" as an answer. (*Anger is not a feeling, folks!*) Maybe you're feeling sad, left out, hurt, minimized or helpless. Tap into those emotions and identify the feeling.

3. Process the activating event (with an "I" statement). Now, share how you feel with your partner through an "I" statement. Some examples might be:
   - "I feel hurt when mean things are said to me."
   - "I feel minimized when I hear a parental tone of voice."
   - "I feel upset that my opinion was not asked or unilateral decisions were made."

4. Wait for validation. After sharing how you really feel, notice your partner's response. Typically, he or she wasn't even aware of how you felt—or else he/she

didn't realize how much it bothered you—and will validate your feelings. I hear many couples who work through this exercise, saying things like:

- "I had no idea that bothered you so much!"
- "I'm sorry, I didn't mean to hurt your feelings."
- "Why didn't you tell me before? I didn't think you'd mind if I did that."

Now, if for some reason your partner does not validate your feelings, don't despair! Simply find ways that you can vent and get those negative emotions out of your system. Hit a pillow, scream into that pillow, or write how you feel in your journal. As I mentioned before, healthy venting will actually make you feel better, because even if your partner isn't acknowledging how you feel, *you* are making that acknowledgement. This alone may be enough to prevent you from entering the tornado.

If you still don't feel better after venting, you may want to consider going back to your partner and sharing your "I" statements again, because it's possible that your partner was triggered at some point, too, and wasn't ready to validate you the first time you shared your feelings.

5. Enjoy the feeling! Enjoy the sensation of relief that comes with being validated—or truly venting the way you feel. If you get stuck and cannot identify your feelings you can find a list of feelings to select from at my website www.DrRandee.com.

In the rare case that this exercise doesn't prevent you from entering the tornado, don't be too hard on yourself. Old, deeply ingrained habits can sometimes be difficult to break and it's possible that if this is a recurring pattern in your relationship, you may need to enlist the help of a skilled therapist to help you practice the process until it becomes comfortable for both of you.

Chapter 15
A Linear Look at Relationships

*"Holding on is believing that there's a past;
letting go is knowing that there's a future.*

- Daphne Rose Kingma

Olivia was engaged years ago to Jaime. The two had everything planned—the dress, the reception hall, everything!—until one day Olivia came home from work only to find a three-page goodbye letter from Jaime. In the letter, he tells Olivia he's spooked and just too young to commit to someone for the rest of his life. Olivia is heartbroken.

Several years later, Olivia meets Brett, a loving, wonderful man. After dating for two years, Brett proposes, and Olivia is ecstatic—until the day Brett says, "Honey, I think we should work on getting a joint bank account. Let's start saving money for us, for our wedding, our future."

Uncharacteristically for Olivia, she retorts with, "No freaking way! Absolutely not!"

Brett has no response; he's dumbfounded. Why did she react like that? *Brett asks himself as he scratches his head in disbelief.*

What went wrong here? Brett's suggestion to open the joint account is eerily similar to the trauma Olivia endured with Jaime, and this is what really triggered her reaction toward Brett. When Jaime called things off with Olivia, the two of them had a joint account. He also emptied the joint bank account and moved back to Canada. Sadly, these reactions—founded on past experiences—are common. This is unhealthy and will definitely put a strain on any relationship over time.

The solution lies in the realization that relationships have a linear nature to them. In other words, if we look chronologically at the "lifespan" of a relationship, we can also add events that predate the current partner—but they can and often do affect the current relational dynamics.

For a couple like Olivia and Brett, I would write A, B, and C on a board. A represents the moment when Brett and Olivia became a couple. Just to the left of the A, I would write "Before Brett" and "Before Olivia."

Before Brett
Before Oliva   A————————B————————C

The line between A and B represents the first time a high-conflict situation occurs within a relationship. Each situation is represented by a circle on this line; for instance, Brett wanting to open a joint checking account. This circle symbolizes some source of contention between Brett and Olivia.

Before Brett
Before Oliva   A••————————B————————C

The goal then, is to "square off" (deal with) each event by keeping it *between the couple* instead of letting the past affect the present. In the case of Olivia and Brett, we would need to examine what causes such a response from Olivia for this situation. By talking through a similar previous experience between Olivia and Jaime, we will understand the origin of Olivia's reaction. Because it is derived from a situation that occurred before her relationship with Brett, we will draw an arrow from this circle to "Before Olivia" and "Before Brett".

With further discussion, Brett says "First of all, I am not Jaime and I really don't care if my name is on the bank account, I just want to start saving together for our wedding." After Olivia hears this, she can delineate Brett from Jaime and start to trust him.

Now that Brett has provided a solution to Olivia's situation, I would then "square off" the current circle on the line between A and B, to demonstrate that this situation now has a resolution based in the here and now, and not on previous experiences.

Let's look at another example of a point between A and B: It's a year into Olivia and Brett's marriage, and things are moving along smoothly until she goes back to graduate school. This catapults Olivia back to her childhood when her mother went back to college and her parents divorced shortly thereafter. Olivia begins to spiral and tell herself, "Oh, my God, I just took this class on ... what if Brett and I end up divorced? Right after my mom went back to school, their marriage fell apart; maybe I'm recreating the same dynamic in our marriage." This would be a new circle on the A to B line.

Olivia says to Brett, "We're going to be divorced, I just know it!" But then Olivia realizes that she's being triggered back to the time before Brett—a time when she couldn't trust anything positive in her life, along with the trigger where she watched other important relationships in her life fall apart. Because this event was triggered by the past, we draw an arrow from this new circle back to the "Before Olivia" and "Before Brett" section.

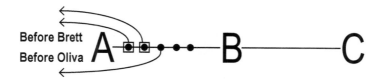

Brett's response? "Well, let's go to therapy together." By understanding the origin of this feeling and understanding how to work through it, we can square off this issue.

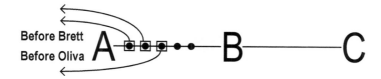

We could continue this process with any other issue Brett and Olivia face that may have been related to their family of origin or previous experiences. Each one of these situations would be a new point on the line.

But what about the line from B to C? This represents a new instance of a similar situation arising within Olivia and Brett's relationship.

For example, a few years later, Brett and Olivia decide to buy a house. Initially, Olivia fears making such a commitment, worried that Brett might abandon her and leave the mortgage all to her. Because this situation is very similar to an issue Olivia and Brett have already faced, it can be represented by a point on the line between B and C.

Now, instead of discussing and examining all the way back to "Before Olivia" and "Before Brett", we can simply draw an arrow back to the similar point on the "A to B" line. Because Olivia has already experienced this sort of conflict before with Brett, the previous instance serves as a new reference point. Olivia can think back on the discussion that allowed them to work through the original event (A to B) and apply that to the new instance (B to C). This is the point where trust is developed.

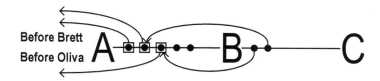

To use a chart or illustration like this allows couples to understand and visualize the potential sources of disagreements or friction they experience. Being able to equate a current event with a previous experience allows the couple to make decisions based on their own current relationship and not based on the past. When a couple establishes these events and works through them based upon the present, they lay the foundation by which future issues can be measured and compared. It is invaluable to use this tool to examine their lives before their relationship. It offers them a more pertinent and relevant reference, rather than starting from scratch each time an issue arises. Working through the B to C line, the couple moves closer to C, the commitment phase—the place where they are totally content with one another.

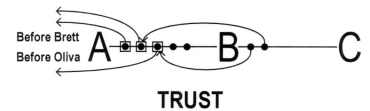

Before Brett
Before Oliva

TRUST
is developed between B and C
when new issues are resolved
by referring back to issues
solved during A to B

Here are two additional examples of how previous experiences can interfere with present situations.

A. Melissa and Sam are married. Sam was married twice before, and both ex-wives cheated on him. In this case, we put "Before Sam" and "Before Melissa" to the left of point A. When Sam finds Melissa emailing and texting pictures to her male friend (Richard)

Sam becomes irate and insecure. This reaction is based upon information from the past, where Sam has had bad experiences with his ex-wives. His feelings have nothing to do with anything related to his time spent with Melissa. This is an overreaction. It is triggered by previous experiences around which he still has much baggage—but all of it predates Melissa.

B. Cathy's mother used to be very controlling. She spoke to Cathy in a very critical tone. When husband Harvey talks to Cathy in a certain tone of voice, it catapults her back to times in childhood of high conflict where her mother tried to control her. Cathy is easily triggered whenever Harvey's tone reminds Cathy of her mother—even though the issues with her mom occurred years before Harvey was in the picture.

EXERCISE: SQUARING OFF
WITH YOUR PAST

This exercise will allow you to understand how your past is affecting your present experiences and relationships. Following the steps listed below will allow you to create a linear view of your own life and determine the sources of high-conflict situations. The more you can separate your present from your past, the easier it becomes to remain in the present, without reliving past dramas and traumas.

1. Think about a time that you became upset with someone recently. Try to look at the situation critically and objectively; is the cause of your reaction based upon the things in the present, or are you taking in information based upon similar experiences you have had in the past? For this exercise, we are looking at any current situation that is drawing on past experiences.

2. For each of the instances you have determined in step 1, draw a circle within the line from A to B. Determine the cause or origin of the issue. Try to think about the previous experience that you are drawing upon in the present to create this situation. Once you have pinpointed the source as an experience from your past, draw an arrow from the circle to the "Before" section to the left of A.

3. Next, determine a course of action that can help address this issue based on present information without drawing on past experiences. For example, Cathy might talk to Harvey and explain why she

doesn't appreciate the tone of voice he uses. They come up with a plan to let Harvey know whenever Cathy feels threatened by this tone. Once a solution has been determined, you can "square off" the circle. This represents the idea that the past experience is no longer the source of the high-conflict situation because you are now able deal with the present situation instead. In other words, the past situation no longer has anything to do with the current situation.

Finally, keep this chart as a reference for any new high-conflict situation you may find yourself in. If you notice a situation arise similar to one already addressed, draw a circle on the line from B to C. Then draw an arrow back to the similar experience you examined on the A to B line. What was the solution then? Because of the similarities, you can draw from this similar experience without having to go all the way back to the "Before" section, keeping the past experiences from interfering with the present.

As you become aware of how easy it is to intertwine the past and present, you will be able to recognize what is happening, prevent past negativity from influencing your present relationships and circumstances or begin the process of uncoupling the past and present (in instances where you've already been triggered). This separation will begin to put the past in its place.

When the past "baggage" is no longer superimposed onto your present, you will see that the present is much more manageable (and less scary, too!). You can't change the past, but you can change the way you choose to react to your present moments.

Chapter 16
Perfection Pie

"Perfectionism is not a quest for the best. It is a pursuit of the worst in ourselves, the part that tells us that nothing we do will ever be good enough - that we should try again."

- Julia Cameron

Xavier and his wife, Maura, are driving home from dinner. They have just spent the evening with another couple, but now that they're alone in the car, Maura refuses to speak to her husband.

"What's wrong, honey?" Xavier asks, even though he has a feeling he already knows. The moment he made that joke at dinner his wife became noticeably silent.

"You know what's wrong! You made that joke about the air-headed blonde woman, and it was obvious that you were referring to me."

Xavier is immediately contrite. "Maura, I'm sorry. It was honestly a joke. I didn't mean to hurt your feelings—"

"Oh, I've heard that excuse a million times before! Xavier, you're always so sarcastic—and it's always at my expense."

At this point, Xavier goes on defense. "Maura, I'm a sarcastic person. What can I say? But you're exaggerating about how often I make a joke about you. In the end, it doesn't really matter; I could make one joke in a million, and you'd somehow find fault with it. You take everything way too seriously."

Clearly Xavier's sarcasm is a thorn in Maura's side. It has escalated to the point that Maura can't let go whenever her husband makes any type of joke. Xavier, on the other hand doesn't see this as an issue, since his intentions are good. He knows in his heart that he rarely makes jokes about his wife—but in her mind, it's a constant occurrence.

When I work with a couple like this—where their perceptions of events are different—I like to use the Perfection Pie exercise:

Perfection Pie

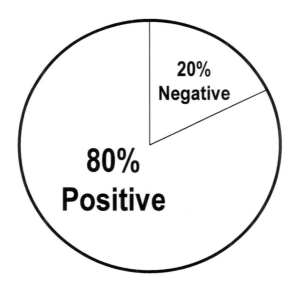

For Xavier and Maura, I drew a circle on the board and asked them what percentage they would assign to the negative aspects of the relationship. They both felt about 20 percent was negative, so I created a wedge representing 20 percent, putting "negative" in that portion to signify the negative share. Then I wrote positive in the 80 percent section to represent the positive qualities of the relationship.

A perfectionist tends to take the negative portion (in this case 20 percent) magnify it and imagine the negative is 100 percent of the pie. Usually when I help people fill in the pie it becomes easy for the perfectionist to identify with this tendency to blow the negative out of proportion. That's exactly what happened with this couple. Maura had written, "He's sarcastic" in the negative section, and Xavier had written "We argue too much—especially about my sarcasm." Maura took one look at the pie that only had two negative statements written in the 20 percent portion and said, "Oh, my God! That's what I do! I get so upset when he makes a joke that in my mind it's 100 percent of our marriage!"

The goal is to learn how to let go of that perfectionism, especially with one's partner. This work will also involve working *with* one another, so that both individuals start focusing on the positive. Working as a team is crucial, because what sometimes happens is the perfectionist has spent so much time blowing the negative aspects out of proportion that the attitude becomes contagious. Over time the other partner—even if he or she isn't a perfectionist—will also begin to perceive the relationship as 100 percent negative. This was starting to happen with Xavier, as he was getting exasperated with the constant criticism.

It is necessary to identify and address the negatives in a partnership. Typically when couples fill out the negative segment I see lists like this:

- *He is impatient.*
- *She can't make up her mind.*
- *He's always late.*

To prevent perfectionism taking over the relationship, I then ask the couple to fill in the positive portion of the pie with very specific information. One couple listed these items in their positive portion of the pie:

- *She's loyal and kind.*
- *He's sensitive and thoughtful.*
- *We both agree on how to raise our children.*
- *We both share some of the same interests (movies, golf, gardening).*
- *We are both hard workers.*
- *He's funny.*
- *She's nurturing with the children.*

As the list grows, couples begin to realize there are so many positives, and many times these lists outweigh the negatives.

It is typical for the negative list to be significantly shorter than the positive one. Once the couple realizes this, everything feels more manageable. They begin to see that while there are aspects of the relationship to work on, it's not as bad as they thought. From this realization it becomes easier to address the negatives with the assurance that the relationship has many more positives that the couple may have been neglecting.

In the event that the negative list begins to grow long, it is important to decide if this is perfectionism coming into play or if the issue is truly bigger than the couple can handle alone. When it's perfectionism, one or both partners are nit-picking and taking the smallest idiosyncrasies and pointing them out. This occurs with people who cannot let go of anything that displeases them, no matter how small. In this instance, they need to spend just as much time finding the many positives in their relationship. They need to hyper-focus on the positive (just as they have scrutinized the negative in the past).

However, if perfectionism isn't the culprit and the negative list is too overwhelming or serious to deal with between them, then it is important for the couple to seek outside counseling or advice. Then they can move ahead in a way that is best for both people. In cases of abuse, addiction, etc., a couple will need more targeted assistance and I would urge them to seek immediate therapeutic services.

Of those couples who think they have all of these terrible issues, many are relieved to see there is actually more good in their relationship than they perhaps originally thought—and that perfectionistic tendencies inflate smaller issues into ones that temporarily overshadow all of the positives.

For Maura and Xavier, this exercise allowed them to work on the sarcastic comments that annoyed Maura, while appreciating all of the wonderful traits each individual brought to the relationship. With time and attention to the positives this specific area of conflict became less important in Maura's eyes: Xavier felt less defensive and he became more attuned and sensitive to the types of jokes that his wife appreciated, as opposed to the remarks that hurt her feelings. And because this couple was open to change, Maura honestly began to enjoy and appreciate her husband's sense of humor!

EXERCISE: MAKE YOUR OWN PIE!

For this exercise, draw a circle on a piece of paper and work with your partner to complete the following steps:

1. Divide the pie into portions that indicate the level of negative and positive proportions of the relationship and label each with a plus and minus sign.

2. Get specific. Fill in each section of the pie by listing all of the positives you see in your partner, as well as the positives you experience as a couple. Do the same for the negative portion.

3. Confront the negative. Look at each item on the negative list, and use the strategies in other chapters of this book that address the issues at hand. For example, if you argue frequently, revisit Chapter Thirteen ("To Argue or Not To Argue"). Or if one person nags the other Chapter Ten ("The Should List") will help.

4. Be positive! Finally, take time to review and appreciate all the positives. Some couples even copy this list onto a separate piece of paper and keep it in a prominent location as a constant reminder of what's good with the relationship.

Chapter 17
The Balance Wheel

"Life is like riding a bicycle. To keep your balance, you must keep moving."

- Albert Einstein

Giovanni loves working out; in fact, it is a part of almost every aspect of his life. As a personal trainer, he spends about ten hours each day at the gym, helping others to reach their fitness goals. At home, he has also been working hard to get his online workout video business off the ground. So far, the online memberships to view his videos have been very successful.

But often on the evenings that he returns to the gym for his own workout, the following conversation with his wife, Karen, unfolds:

"Giovanni, where are you going?"

"To the gym!"

"But you were there all day ... "

"Yeah, but that isn't a workout for me. This is my workout time."

Karen scowls and points to the crib. "What about time with the baby?"

"Oh, honey, you know I play with her when I get home from work. And I always do the late feeding so you can sleep."

Karen laughs sarcastically. "Gee, thanks. I spend almost every hour of the day taking care of our daughter, with no time to work out. You know I love her, but when do I get time for me?"

TO THIS, GIOVANNI HAS NO ANSWER.

This situation is a classic issue of imbalance, and although some of this comes from each individual, it contributes to overall relationship issues. Both partners in this case are out of balance; they spend way too much time on one aspect of their lives while the other areas suffer as a result. Karen spends many hours each day caring for their baby, and Giovanni spends most of his time working out, helping others work out, or working on his workout business.

Although there's absolutely nothing wrong with wanting to support the family and enjoy physical fitness (in the case of Giovanni) or wanting to give plenty of time and attention to a young child (in Karen's instance), the fact that both individuals aren't allotting any time to other aspects of their lives has culminated in hurt feelings, arguments and a relational impasse.

So, how can a couple like Karen and Giovanni improve their relationship? First, they need to spend some time on getting themselves balanced. For this, they will benefit from The Balance Wheel.

THE BALANCE WHEEL

The balance wheel is a representation of the four main areas in life that provide balance and fulfillment: mental, spiritual, physical and emotional.

BALANCE WHEEL

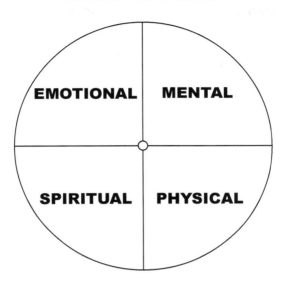

All of the people, activities, hobbies, etc. in your life then become the "spokes" of the wheel. For Giovanni, he is clearly filling up the "physical" quadrant of the wheel with the following spokes: personal training job, online training videos and working out six days a week.

Giovanni's Wheel

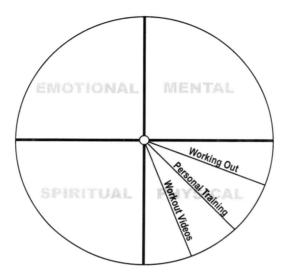

Karen, on the other hand, has lots of spokes in the emotional category: baby, family, Giovanni and a new moms' group.

Karen's Wheel

Giovanni can certainly add "baby" and "Karen" to his emotional spokes, but that's about all he has time for in his life, since his businesses consume the rest of his time. Also note that neither partner feels that they have any appreciable spokes in the mental and spiritual categories at this point in their lives.

If this were a real wheel it would be unstable. When there are not enough spokes in one quadrant and outside stressors or forces interact with the wheel, it will go flat. In order to feel balanced and resilient it is important to aim for a full wheel with at least three spokes in each quadrant. Then, when an outside stressor enters your world, you will simply ride over it. If Karen and Giovanni could shore up the spokes in all parts of their respective wheels, then the wheels would be impervious to the typical stresses and strains of life: limited time, demands from family members, loss of income if business slows down, a sick child, etc.

But until the two of them can each create more balanced wheels, any areas of weakness in their lives are sure to create conflicts for them as a couple. When both wheels are complete, couples can connect their wheels and ride together towards balance.

WHEEL BALANCING

To begin balancing their wheels, I would ask Karen what stimulates her mentally. She might say, "I used to read books and attend a local book club, but I don't have time—or else I'm too tired." To that I would suggest that perhaps Karen's mother would help her with evening babysitting once a week (instead of during the day) so Karen could take a nap and then read and/or attend book club meetings. After creating several mental spokes, we would do the same for the spiritual and physical areas.

To balance Giovanni's poorly balanced wheel, he may decide to do yoga once a week for spiritual nourishment in lieu of his normal workout routine. For emotional stimulation, he might head out once a week to have lunch and connect with friends. He would then continue to add to his spokes until each quadrant has at least three spokes in it.

WHEEL ALIGNMENT

When Giovanni and Karen both have balanced wheels, they will have created enough strength in the spokes so that if they experience troubles or hit a bump, they can metaphorically just roll over those bumps and keep moving. The reality is most people don't balance their wheels and as soon as they hit a problem area, their tire quickly deflates and they are stuck. This is why people get stressed out, depressed, angry or despondent.

Sometimes one of the pair may try to create balance and borrow a spoke from the other one's wheel. Let's say Karen starts to work out with Giovanni. She does it because he loves it so much but she finds she does not really enjoy it. This is rarely a successful strategy. Karen needs her own spoke! Maybe for her, she discovers a Mommy & Me class that is more physical, but still gives her time to bond with the baby; now she hasn't sacrificed her emotional life, yet her wheel is quickly re-balancing.

As couples begin to come to the relationship with their own balanced wheels then there is a strong connection—almost as if those wheels have an axle connecting them so they can roll together through life. The goal for couples, then, is to create a full wheel for each individual and connect with a partner who also has a full wheel. Otherwise, one person may feel pressure to overcompensate for the weaknesses in his or her partner's wheel, and that typically results in resentment from the partner who feels that he or she is "doing all the work."

BALANCE WHEEL

However, with two balanced wheels, when either or both experiences something negative, they can both roll with it, bump over it and deal with it.

EXERCISE: CREATE YOUR OWN BALANCE WHEEL

Now it's time for you to fill in the spokes in your life and determine how balanced your wheel is. I suggest you ask your partner to complete the exercise as well. Create your wheels separately and then afterwards you'll have a chance to share with one another. Remember that you can't use the same spoke in more than one quadrant.

1. Emotional: Begin with your emotional quadrant and draw your first spoke with a line from the center out to the edge. Ask yourself, "What is something that touches my soul, my heart? Is there anyone in my life that I engage with who touches me emotionally? What do I do for myself daily that fulfills me emotionally?" These connections could include friends, pets, children, other family members and your partner. Label each item you have placed in the emotional quadrant, as shown in the illustration.

2. Mental: Draw spokes in the mental quadrant. Think about what you do for yourself that is mentally stimulating on a daily basis. It could be reading, watching educational shows, taking classes, watching a TED talk online or anything else mentally interesting. Now label each item you placed in this quadrant as you did with the emotional quadrant.

3. Spiritual: When considering your spiritual quadrant, include any activities that support your spiritual development. Activities like yoga and meditation can provide you with spiritual nourishment. Other spiritual items may include: any worship you do in a church, synagogue, mosque, meeting house, etc.; spiritual or

inspirational reading; workshops; audios and videos. Be sure to label each item you have place in this quadrant.

4. Physical: Working out, running, skiing, walking, swimming—anything that gets your heart pumping falls into this category! Remember that there are activities—like gardening—that aren't always thought of as traditional sports or workouts but would count here. Just as you have with the other quadrants, be sure to label each spoke you have placed in it.

5. Evaluate your quadrants: Now, take a look at each quadrant. Imagine your wheel rolling through a rocky terrain. Is there any place on the wheel that seems weaker or thinner, more likely to crack against the bumps? Any area with three spokes is strong enough to support that quadrant of the wheel, so if you see any that have less then that, those might be quadrants that could use some fortification. Don't be alarmed if one of your quadrants has a few too many spokes. Three is enough to support the wheel, one or two more serve to add more strength behind that quadrant. However, it is also important to consider that having too many spokes in one quadrant can cause the wheel to become unwieldy and off-balanced, especially if the other quadrants are lacking.

6. Fill in weak quadrants: If you find that certain quadrants have less than three spokes, begin adding ideas and activities that can fill these areas. If you're stuck, ask yourself, "What did I like to do before I was in a

relationship (or before children)? What really stimulates me? What do I like to do? What are my interests?"
Make a list of spokes that you may want to add in any
quadrant that is not complete.

7.   Share: Now it's time to share your wheels; check for
areas where you share common items, and look to the
differences to take time to appreciate what makes your
partner special (and vice-versa). The wheels don't have
to be identical—just balanced. From this position, you
can prevent many problems and when the inevitable
difficulties in life arise, both of you are in a position
to deal with the issues head-on, from a healthy and
balanced perspective.

Chapter 18
Family of Origin Board

"Everything that irritates us about others can lead us to an understanding of ourselves."

- Carl Jung

FAMILY OF ORIGIN

The *Family of Origin Board* is a comprehensive exercise that explores the depth of the messages you received from your parents, as well as the beliefs, attitudes and patterns of behavior you still carry with you. It clearly identifies what you may still be carrying emotionally, and the personality traits that you have developed as a result of the many complex interactions you have had with your own family of origin. The *Family of Origin Board* will show you the following:

- How you learned what love is
- How you learned to be loved
- What emotions you still carry from your childhood
- What personality traits you may or may not have that are different from your parents

- How individuated you are from your parents
- How emotionally available your parents were for you
- Rules of loving: those that you learned and those you have unlearned
- Why you chose your partner
- Why you feel stuck or frustrated in your relationship
- Why you do what you do—and how to stop behaviors that no longer serve you, and
- How to be more understanding of your mate once you learn how he or she was raised.

I designed the *Family of Origin Board* for couples so that they could understand each other better. It helps them explore the reasons they may be struggling and why they may be emotionally stuck. Couples who have completed this exercise state that it was a huge awakening for them. They say it is a powerful and eye-opening experience—one that helps them be more patient and kind toward one another.

The good news is that you do not have to be involved in a relationship to complete a *Family of Origin Board*. That's because this exercise teaches you:

1. What to look out for in a relationship
2. What you need to work on personally to become and/or remain emotionally healthy, and
3. How *not* to repeat dysfunctional patterns.

Teens can also benefit from this board. It helps them see what their parents are like and why, and it helps them as they move toward greater autonomy. More importantly it gives them perspective on how they want to be in a relationship and gives them a head start in cultivating healthy relationships with others.

AN INVITATION:

Due to the in-depth nature of the *Family of Origins Board* exercise, as well as the strong emotional reactions that may result, this exercise is best completed with the help of an experienced guide. To learn more about this transformative exercise or schedule an appointment to begin this work, please visit www.DrRandee.com. Couples, individuals and teens are all welcome.

About the Author

Dr. Randee Anderson is a highly sought-after therapist who specializes in working with couples and relationship issues. Since the early 1990s Dr. Anderson has been helping couples experience more joy and love while showing them how to significantly reduce conflict and change dysfunctional behaviors.

Approaching each client with kindness, clarity and compassion, Dr. Anderson has the rare gift of being able to shine light on why a couple has a problem while at the same time providing pragmatic steps that lead to deeper love for themselves and their partner.

In addition to her doctorate in psychology, Dr. Anderson also has earned two master's degrees, one in Marriage, Family, and Child Therapy and one in Education.

To learn more about Dr. Anderson visit her website at: www.DrRandee.com